British Trade Unions since 1933

This textbook reviews major issues concerning the history of British trade unions in the last two-thirds of the twentieth century. Even with the decline in membership of the 1980s and 1990s, trade unions in Britain have remained the largest voluntary organisations in the country and the total membership has remained larger than in most other countries. The book discusses many major aspects of trade unionism and many controversies concerning it, including strikes (often seen as a peculiarly 'British disease'). Trade union presence in the labour market has been deemed a cause of higher unemployment and lower productivity. The trade unions have been accused of being insensitive on gender and ethnicity. They have also been accused of being corporatist, unelected partners in government (especially in the 1940–79 period). Overall, this book gives students a lucid and up-to-date introduction to the recent history of British trade unionism.

CHRIS WRIGLEY is Professor of Modern British History at the University of Nottingham. He is author or editor of numerous books on political and labour history, most recently *The First World War and the International Economy* (2000).

New Studies in Economic and Social History

Edited for the Economic History Society by
Maurice Kirby
Lancaster University

This series, specially commissioned by the Economic History Society, provides a guide to the current interpretations of the key themes of economic and social history in which advances have recently been made or in which there has been significant debate.

In recent times economic and social history has been one of the most flourishing areas of historical study. This has mirrored the increasing relevance of the economic and social sciences both in a student's choice of career and in forming a society at large more aware of the importance of these issues in their everyday lives. Moreover, specialist interests in business, agricultural and welfare history, for example, have themselves burgeoned and there has been an increased interest in the economic development of the wider world. Stimulating as these scholarly developments have been for the specialist, the rapid advance of the subject and the quantity of new publications make it difficult for the reader to gain an overview of particular topics, let alone the whole field.

New Studies in Economic and Social History is intended for students and their teachers. It is designed to introduce them to fresh topics and to enable them to keep abreast of recent writing and debates. All the books in the series are written by a recognised authority in the subject, and the arguments and issues are set out in a critical but unpartisan fashion. The aim of the series is to survey the current state of scholarship, rather than to provide a set of pre-packaged conclusions.

The series has been edited since its inception in 1968 by Professors M. W. Flinn, T. C. Smout and L. A. Clarkson, and is currently edited by Professor Maurice Kirby. From 1968 it was published by Macmillan as Studies in Economic History, and after 1974 as Studies in Economic and Social History. From 1995 New Studies in Economic and Social History is being published on behalf of the Economic History Society by Cambridge University Press. This new series includes some of the titles previously published by Macmillan as well as new titles, and reflects the ongoing development throughout the world of this rich seam of history.

For a full list of titles in print, please see the end of the book.

British Trade Unions since 1933

Prepared for the Economic History Society by

Chris Wrigley
University of Nottingham

331. 8809 42
W 95b

PUBLISHED BY THE PRESS SYNDICATE OF THE UNIVERSITY OF CAMBRIDGE
The Pitt Building, Trumpington Street, Cambridge CB2 1RP, United Kingdom

CAMBRIDGE UNIVERSITY PRESS
The Edinburgh Building, Cambridge, CB2 2RU, UK
40 West 20th Street, New York, NY 10011-4211, USA
477 Williamstown Road, Port Melbourne, VIC 3207, Australia
Ruiz de Alarcón 13, 28014 Madrid, Spain
Dock House, The Waterfront, Cape Town 8001, South Africa

http://www.cambridge.org

© The Economic History Society 2002

First published 2002

Printed in the United Kingdom at the University Press, Cambridge

Typeface Plantin 10/12.5 pt   *System* LaTeX 2_ε [TB]

MIL *A catalogue record for this book is available from the British Library*

Library of Congress Cataloguing in Publication data

Wrigley, Chris.
British Trade Unions since 1933 / prepared for the Economic History
Society by Chris Wrigley.
    p.   cm. – (New Studies in Economic and Social History; 46)
Includes bibliographical references and index.
ISBN 0 521 57231 2 (hardback) –ISBN 0 521 57640 7 (paperback)
1. Labor unions – Great Britain – History – 20th century.   I. Title.
II. Series.

HD6664 .W753   2002
331.88'0941 – DC21   2002067379

ISBN 0 521 57231 2 hardback
ISBN 0 521 57640 7 paperback

Contents

Tables

Chapter 1

Introduction

In Britain both the fortunes and the public standing of the trade unions fluctuated markedly in the final two-thirds of the twentieth century. The trade unions gained much kudos in the 1940s for their role in helping to mobilise the British economy for war and for post-war economic recovery. Thereafter, as the British economy performed relatively poorly among industrialised nations, the trade unions received much blame for numerous economic 'British diseases', including a proneness to strike and low productivity.

Other than during the First and Second World Wars and their immediate aftermaths, British industrial relations, from at least the late nineteenth century to the 1970s, were based primarily on a willingness of employers and working people's representatives to settle differences on a voluntary basis. The two world wars boosted the spread of collective bargaining and, especially, national collective bargaining. Where major industrial confrontations occurred, or seemed likely, the government (through the Board of Trade, the Ministry of Labour and its successors) could intervene, if both parties were agreeable, and offer suggested solutions to disputes. Such action was authorised under the Conciliation Act, 1896 and the Industrial Courts Act, 1919. Compared with other countries, Britain's peacetime system of industrial relations until the 1970s was untrammelled by legal constraints, the Trade Disputes Act, 1906 having given trade unions immunity from legal actions for damages and strengthened their rights to peaceful picketing.

The British trade union movement, which had been steeped in Liberalism until the late nineteenth century and beyond, was overwhelmingly against interference with free collective bargaining. For its leaders this was a principle clearly won through past struggles and on a par with free speech in a free society. In contrast, for at least three decades after the Second World War, they advocated planning in the economy other than in the labour market. Free market economists and many Conservatives argued for the opposite: no interference with private enterprise but restrictions on trade unionism (on the grounds of it being an impediment to free market forces).

Political arguments concerning trade unionism in Britain, as in many other countries, were coloured by the unions' role in politics. The Trades Union Congress (TUC) had set up the Labour Party (or, to be precise, its predecessor, the Labour Representation Committee) in 1900. Before the First World War over 95 per cent of Labour Party members were affiliated through the trade unions, there being then no direct individual members. The trade unions provided the bulk of the Labour Party's finances then and later, especially before the mid-1990s. For instance, in 1990 trade union affiliation fees provided two-thirds of the party's regular annual income. Not surprisingly, the role of the trade unions in industrial relations was a major issue in British politics for much of the twentieth century.

Renewed criticism of the trade unions was particularly notable from the early to mid-1950s, a period when there were growing anxieties about inflation and Britain's competitiveness as a trading nation as well as about strikes. By the 1960s both the Conservative and Labour Parties were proposing political solutions to deal with industrial relations problems which, explicitly or implicitly, centred on trade unionism. The 'trade union issue' remained prominent until the mid-1990s; by which time adverse economic conditions, reinforced by legislation and more generally by a political climate hostile to the trade unions, had considerably weakened trade unionism. Moreover, Tony Blair, the leader of the Labour Party (from 1994) and Prime Minister (from 1997), took pains to distance the Labour Party from the TUC and the trade unions (though the Labour Party remained more sympathetic to many trade union concerns than the Conservatives).

There were also other types of criticism of the trade unions. In the radical ethos of the 1960s and early 1970s their position was often ambiguous. While many trade union leaders and activists readily marched for peace in Vietnam, on behalf of Biafra in the war in Nigeria, for civil rights in Northern Ireland, against apartheid in South Africa and the Smith regime in Rhodesia, for CND and Amnesty International as well as other causes of the time, the trade unions collectively appeared male dominated, old-fashioned, even bricks in the wall of the British establishment. The ambiguity lay in the fact that, not surprisingly, trade unions defended jobs in the arms industries, in nuclear power and in producing exports to many (but not all) unsavoury regimes. Moreover, the unions were conspicuously poor on gender and ethnic issues and in appealing to youth.

In the 1960s there were several trade union moves to appeal beyond materialism. One revealing episode concerned the arts. Here again, in an example of the ambiguity of the trade unions as radical or conservative (with a small 'c') bodies, support for radical theatre and films had been a past feature of British socialism, the British co-operative movement, mining and other working-class communities. At the 1960 TUC the General Council suffered a defeat when delegates voted in favour of a motion (number 42 on the agenda) moved by the Association of Cinematograph, Television and Allied Technicians (ACTT) and seconded by the National Union of Mineworkers:

Congress recognises the importance of the arts in the life of the community, especially now when many unions are securing a shorter working week and greater leisure time for their members. It notes that the trade union movement has participated to only a small extent in the direct promotion and encouragement of plays, films, music, literature and other forms of expression, including those of value to its beliefs and principles. Congress considers that much more could be done.

(Trade Union Congress, *Report 1960*, 435)

The impetus for this motion came from the playwright Arnold Wesker. After its success Centre 42 (1961–70) evolved from Wesker's discussions with other intellectuals including Shelagh Delaney, Clive Exton, Bernard Kops and Doris Lessing. At the 1961 TUC an ACTT delegate said of Centre 42 that it was

a voluntary alliance of artists in the field of music, drama, cinema, art and literature. Its aim is to narrow the gap between the artists and the public and to stimulate cultural and artistic activities in the closest association with the trade unions. It hopes to create a permanent centre in London, but equally it intends to duplicate its work in the provincial centres. It is already working in the closest association with a number of trades councils in the organisation of local festivals of art and labour.

(Trade Union Congress, *Report 1961*, 453)

In 1961 a four-day festival of the arts was organised by Welling-borough Trades Council at a cost of £500. In 1962 festival weeks were backed by trades councils in Birmingham, Bristol, Hayes, Leicester, Nottingham and Wellingborough, at a cost of some £50,000 (Wesker, 1970).

The enthusiasm for Centre 42 came from the trades councils, with a few trade union leaders being active supporters. The General Council of the TUC collectively resisted such moves, arguing that there were other sources of support for the arts (notably the state, local government and voluntary bodies), that the trade unions already backed the Workers' Education Association and that (rightly) it would prove to be very costly. A closer look at the views of some of the TUC supporters of motion 42 reveals that some were motivated to hold back the tide of the rock and roll and 'Yankee films' by offering arts and culture to young people. W. Whitehead of the South Wales miners declared:

We are not satisfied in South Wales . . . that culture and art mean rock 'n' roll, the sorcerer's window, *Yogi Bear*, and *Rawhide*, with bluinite detergent. I think . . . our heritage is William Morris, Shakespeare, Shaw and, in the field of music, Vaughn Williams and today Benjamin Britten.

A delegate from the Transport Salaried Staff's Association denounced the flood of 'glossy backed publications with lurid covers . . . of sex and violence' and more generally the 'overwhelming glut of distorted degradation' (Trade Union Congress, *Report 1960*, 438). Clearly, for some, culture was something of a rearguard action against American commercialism.

Centre 42 itself was criticised by more radical cultural groups later in the 1960s for taking culture to the workers in an elitist manner. There was less criticism of much of later union sponsorship of political plays in the 1970s and after. For example, the Transport and General Workers' Union sponsored *The Non-Stop Connolly Show* in Dublin, London and elsewhere in 1975. The Amalgamated Union of Engineering Workers and its white-collar associate, Technical and Supervisory Section (TASS) were linked to *Happy Robots*, a play concerning automation at work which was put on in 1973 by Red Ladder (Itzin, 1980).

The early enthusiasm for Centre 42 was centred on trades councils, which by the later decades of the twentieth century were the recognised local subsidiaries of the TUC. The local trade union activists who were delegates to these bodies often put in long hours promoting trade unionism, providing trade union inputs into a range of local matters from allotments committees to community relations councils and supporting various demonstrations. While the tabloid press made much of 'wicked NUPE (National Union of Public Employees) shop stewards' during the 'winter of discontent, 1979', at the local level there was often much respect for them, especially for overworked nurses who campaigned for better funding of the National Health Service and backed the several TUC sponsored People's Marches for Jobs.

In the 1980s, as in the 1930s, trade union activism often proved self-sacrificing. In economic recessions employers often made shop stewards and part-time union officials redundant. In good times trade union activities involved less family and leisure time and little if any economic reward. Yet men and women took on various tasks in a belief that they were bettering their own and their colleagues' lot.

The view from the shop floor and from the office has been much less written about than the view from the TUC or the national headquarters of major unions. In surveying major issues in the literature on British trade unionism this book is mostly a national-level account.

In this short study of British trade unions in the period 1933–2000 the focus is on some major post-Second World War themes, with a chapter as a prologue on 1933–45. The make-up of trade union membership changed very markedly between the Second World War and the turn of the century, with the unions representing less industrial male workers but more women and male white-collar workers, and generally being stronger in the public than the private sector of the economy. The trade unions had to make greater efforts to provide attractive services to their members in the harsher economic and political climate after 1979. Moreover, they needed to demonstrate their members' support, and in particular for political funds and for strike action, under the legislation of 1980–1993. In other chapters government intervention in the form of prices and incomes policies and trade union law are examined and also the controversies concerning strikes and the economic effects of trade unions.

At the start of the twenty-first century the trade unions had experienced a substantial drop in membership and had become accustomed to less influence in Whitehall and Westminster than they had enjoyed in 1946–79. Nevertheless, the trade unions remained a major force in Britain, still very substantial in size relative to, say, France and other countries. In 1933–2000, as in previous centuries, the trade unions had to adapt to changing conditions, with a different composition of their membership, and offering a differing mix of services to their members.

Chapter 2

Economic recovery and war, 1933–1945

British trade unions emerged from the Second World War with both their size and their political and social status enhanced. There is not much controversy about that. But there is less recognition of the scale of the recovery of trade union membership, 1933–9, and there is controversy as to the extent to which governments consulted trade unions and its significance.

The world recession of 1931–3 hit British trade unionism less hard than that of 1921–2. In 1920 British trade unionism was stronger than it was to be again until 1974 in terms of trade union density (the percentage of trade union members in the workforce legally eligible to join a union) or, in crude membership numbers, until 1946. In the earlier period trade union membership tumbled from 8,253,000, a 48.2 per cent density in 1920 to 5,382,000, a 30.7 per cent density, in 1923. In contrast, the drop in trade union membership was much less in the early 1930s, from 4,783,000, 25.7 per cent density in 1930 to 4,350,000, 22.9 per cent density in 1933. In other words, the 1917–20 boom in trade unionism was substantially undercut in 1921–2 and subsequent years, while trade union membership had a lesser height from which to fall in 1930–3. That said, trade union density at its inter-war nadir at 22.9 per cent was only lower than that of 1913–14 of the years before the First World War (and much higher than the 16.2 per cent average of 1904–13).

The 1930s have been painted as an unduly dark period for the trade unions. G. D. H. Cole and Raymond Postgate, in their formerly influential *The Common People 1746–1946*, 4th edition, 1949, wrote of the early 1930s: 'For the time being the trade unions could only hang on as best they could, avoiding disputes wherever possible and making practically no attempt to extend their organisation to new groups or industries' (496). In contrast, later writing has emphasised more trade union recovery and its limited but real successes during the 1930s.

There was a substantial recovery of trade union membership. By 1939 it had reached 6,206,000, a density of 31.9 per cent, which put it back to the 1921–2 level, a high level (but not to the exceptional boom level of 1917–20) (Bain and Price, 1980). There was marked growth in some hitherto relatively weak areas. In food and drink union density rose from 14.9 to 23.7 per cent, in clothing from 12.3 to 23.6 per cent and in distribution 7.1 to 11.8 per cent. There were other sectors where unionisation reached new levels, such as road transport (from 47.3 to 68.4 per cent) and footwear (54.7 to 63.4 per cent). There was also recovery in sectors deeply involved in the general strike: coal (52.4 to 81.1 per cent), rail (56.9 to 67.2 per cent) and printing (43.0 to 51.4 per cent). However, there were sectors where union density recovered a little but in a declining labour force, such as cotton (51.4 to 54.4 per cent).

Overall, this was a recovery of trade union membership along traditional lines. There was no substantial increase in female trade union membership, union density rising slower (12.1 to 16.0 per cent) than for male workers (27.9 to 39.3 per cent). It was also marked by white collar unionisation growing a little less strongly than among manual workers. This is a marked contrast to the later decades of the twentieth century.

The 1930s were also not as bad in terms of wages and working hours for those trade unionists still in work as had been the early 1920s. Wage rates fell to an inter-war low in June 1933, but the fall from 1930 to 1933 was from 33.2 to 31.8 (on a wages index with 1956 = 100), whereas the dramatic fall had occurred in the early 1920s after the First World War and its post-war boom, when the index fell from 53.1 in 1920 to 33.5 in 1923. By January 1937 wage rates had passed this 1923 level and were at 35.5 by mid-1939. There was also some recovery of shorter hours of work, albeit small, by 1939 (according to Ministry of Labour statistics on a weekly hours of work index with 1956 = 100, dropping from 108.3 to 107.7) (Employment, Department of, 1968).

The 1930s saw a major and, for the most part, a lasting gain of annual paid holidays for many workers. The TUC had promoted these from 1911 and many workers had secured them during the post-war boom of 1919–20, but for a lot it was a temporary gain (Russell, 1991). The piecemeal achievement of paid holidays is well illustrated by the Shop Assistants Union. By mid-1923 it had secured holiday with pay agreements with 78 Scottish co-operative retail societies, 61 through collective bargaining, 11 via an arbitration award and six by an industrial court award. It also had agreements with 27 firms in London, Glasgow, Leicester and elsewhere. Other trade unions, including engineering, coal, boot and shoe and printing, also had some agreements in the mid-1920s (Hallsworth Papers, Modern Record Centre, Warwick). By 1929 some 1.5 million wage earners were covered. The spread of annual paid holidays quickened in the 1930s. The International Labour Organisation (ILO) adopted a general convention on the subject in June 1936 and the National Government set up a committee of inquiry under Lord Amulree in March 1937. This estimated that 7.75 million workers earning under £250 a year enjoyed annual holidays and recommended that trade boards should be empowered to require paid holidays as well as minimum wages be given to low-paid workers. This proposal was carried out with the Holidays with Pay Act, 1938. By 1943 those receiving holidays with pay were estimated to have nearly doubled to 15 million workers.

As Hugh Clegg has observed: 'the National government... proved to be much more beneficial to the unions and their members once the worst of the economic crisis was over' than had been the Second Labour government (Clegg, 1994, 423). He also observed that 'the 1930s, must be one of the most productive periods of state intervention in industrial relations', pointing from 1933 to the Road and Rail Traffic Act, 1933, the Road Haulage Wages Act, 1938, the Cotton Manufacturing Industry (Temporary Provisions) Act 1934, the Holidays with Pay Act, 1938 and the setting up of trade boards for rubber, furniture and baking (Clegg, 1994, 92–3). In the tradition of Disraeli's social reforms (1874–6) the measures were limited in their extent but nevertheless did represent increased state activity. The Road and Rail Traffic Act, 1933, was in accord with the government's policies to rationalise competition but the only substantial benefit for labour was that it laid down that when the Industrial Court determined fair wages it should take into account existing collective agreements. It did, however, specify maximum hours of work for drivers (Smith, 1997, 65). The Road Haulage Wages Act, 1938, followed the collapse of a wage scheme agreed by the National Joint Conciliation Board for the Road Transport Industry and the recommendations of the Bailie Committee of Inquiry. It set up a statutory framework for the industry through the Road Haulage Central Wages board. As Hugh Clegg and Paul Smith separately have observed, these developments were state sponsored, with the willingness of the employers' associations (in order to stop competitors undercutting their members), not pressure from the trade unions, being the key determinant of the National Government acting (Clegg, 1994, 91–2; Smith, 1997, 78).

Both employers' organisations and trade unions claimed to have successfully influenced the National Government. The British Employers' Federation pointed to its influence over the formation and the financial management of Unemployment Assistance Boards, while the TUC claimed to have had a substantial role in determining the nature of the Workmen's Compensation Act, 1934, and in the introduction of the forty-hour week in government as well as securing the setting up of the Bailie inquiry into holidays with pay. Keith Middlemas, in his influential *Politics In Industrial Society* (1979), observed of these developments,

The fact that right of access to central government did not necessarily convey power needs to be underlined, as does the fundamental failing of employers or union central organisations to deliver bargains binding on their members – still in government eyes a bar to any reciprocal arrangement.

On the other hand, both institutions held government in a net whose meshes, if not strong, were at least numerous. The 1930s witnessed a remarkable proliferation of committees and bodies staffed by the same small group of individuals.

(Middlemas, 1979, 226)

However, Rodney Lowe and others have contested Middlemas' broader argument that British governments after the First World War exhibited 'corporate bias'. Middlemas claimed that the involvement of unelected employers' organisations and trade unions in government decision-making after the First World War turned them into 'governing institutions' and contributed to Britain's social stability. For the inter-war years, Lowe has argued convincingly that the employers' organisations and trade unions were not strong enough for the government to need them, not least as social stability was not under serious threat after 1919–21, but rather the organisations desired 'regular contact with the government to validate their status and so assert authority over their membership' (Lowe, 1987, 197–8). While there is no widespread support for the view that there was substantial 'corporate bias', let alone corporatism, in inter-war Britain, nevertheless there was more consultation of both sides of industry from the mid-1930s economic recovery, and moves to more rapid rearmament to the Second World War.

The pace of rearmament depended very much on political will. It also depended on mobilising resources, not least skilled labour. Early on, in late 1935, government planners assumed that 'consultation with the trade unions will be necessary', but the government preferred to let employers and trade unions in building and engineering resolve their industries' problems of labour shortages. In engineering the Amalgamated Engineering Union's opposition to dilution of labour (using semi- or unskilled labour on hitherto skilled labour's work) was very strong and agreement with the employers was only reached in the summer of 1939. The trade unions feared that the 'armament-fed boom' would be followed by a major economic slump. Nevertheless, the dominant trade union figures of the time, Ernest Bevin, general secretary of the Transport and General Workers' Union, and Walter Citrine, Secretary of the TUC, were eager to help achieve rearmament and did offer ministers help (Parker, 1981; Lowe, 1987).

While trade union membership revived, 1933–9, trade unionism's renewed strength was not generally displayed in strikes. There was an absence of national strikes called between the 1920s and the 1955 rail strike. The numbers of days lost through strikes in 1933–9 were at the lowest for a seven-year period since statistics have been kept, averaging 1,703,000 per annum, only rivalled by part of the 1990s. Coal-mining disputes accounted for nearly half of the days lost (48.6 per cent). Recent analysis by Roy Church and Quentin Outram indicates that in 1927–40, 92 per cent of strikes affected only one colliery and only 4 per cent affected more than one (the rest being unknown), with 46 per cent of the strikes occurring in Scotland and 24 per cent in South Wales (Church and Outram, 1998, 78–82).

Yet there was still bitterness on occasions in industrial relations. This was illustrated in the Harworth dispute of 1936–7, which was notable for violence in a colliery company village. The strike centred on dissatisfaction with the break-away Spencer Union and the call to recognise the Nottingham Miners' Association, and was led by a Communist Party of Great Britain (CPGB) activist, Mick Kane. Stanley Baldwin called for peace at Harworth, saying: 'What is the alternative to collective bargaining? There is none except anarchy... another alternative is force, but we may rule out force in this country.' (Fishman, 1995; Gilbert, 1996b, 170–6).

Communist involvement in disputes was always highlighted, not least by the CPGB. The influence of the CPGB in industrial relations was greater than the size of its membership within the trade unions. In February 1927, according to the CPGB's figures, of a membership of 7,909, 5,823 were trade union members. Of these 3,753 (nearly two-thirds) were in the Miners' Federation of Great Britain, with 219 in the Amalgamated Engineering Union, 168 in the National Union of Railwaymen and 152 in the Transport and General Workers' Union (Worley, 2002, 28). Not surprisingly two of the most influential trade union leaders who were communists – Arthur Horner and Will Paynter – were miners.

While CPGB 'unofficial' activity in the 1930s has received much attention, notably with the London Busmen's Rank and File Movement, formed in 1932, and the Aircraft Shop Stewards' National Council, set up in 1935, the CPGB role in boosting trade union membership should not be overlooked. This included recruiting in notably difficult areas, such as cars and other 'new industries' in the Midlands and the South (Morgan, 1989, 37–8).

The trade unions played a major role in the war effort, especially under Churchill's premiership. Churchill, in the autumn of 1937, had taken considerable pains to strengthen his contacts with the trade union movement. On 3 October 1937 he had written to Anthony Eden: 'Without the support of trade unions our munition programme cannot be properly executed' (Gilbert, 1983, Companion, vol. 5.3, 774–5). In September 1941 he paid tribute to the role of the unions in the war, commenting: 'I... can never forget the support and encouragement which the trade unions, themselves in the forefront of the battle, gave in the darkest days in 1940 and are giving with all their heart today.' Churchill made the leading trade unionist, Ernest Bevin, general secretary of the Transport and General Workers' Union, Minister of Labour and National Service (with a place in the war cabinet from October 1940). George Isaacs, Bevin's successor in Attlee's government, and also a leading trade unionist, later wrote that, 'Bevin, as Minister of Labour, was a necessary condition for the partnership' between Churchill and the trade unions, as 'in Bevin they had a personality who could meet the Prime Minister on level terms' (Wrigley, 2001). Bevin succeeded in playing, as Alan Bullock has pointed out, a dual role: being both 'the representative of the trade unions and the working class in the Cabinet and the spokesman of the government to organised labour' (Bullock, 1967, 4).

As in the First World War, labour's bargaining position in the economy was greatly strengthened by the huge demands of war and by the withdrawal of millions of people into the Armed Forces. In 1940 16.4 per cent of the working population was in the Armed Forces, a percentage which increased to 23.5 per cent in 1945. In January 1940 an interdepartmental committee estimated that in addition to replacing those who went into the Armed Forces, an additional 1,300,000 (70 per cent) people would be needed for munitions, and nearly 2,200,000 (117 per cent) more by July 1941. By the summer of 1941 the long-predicted labour shortages were very evident, with additional need for labour being met by mobilising more women. The National Service (No. 2) Act of 18 December 1941 made all men and women (other than married women living apart from their husbands or women looking after children under 14) liable to undertake national service, whether full or part-time.

Labour was not free to make the most of its potential strength in the wartime labour market. As in the First World War, there was a range of powers enacted to enable the government to achieve more effective use of labour. A Schedule of Reserved Occupations was drawn up before the outbreak of war (whereas one had been brought in in 1917 in the First World War). Also, early on in the war, the government acted to stop employers outbidding one another for skilled labour by the Control of Employment Act, 1939, and the Minister of Labour and National Service was given very wide powers by Regulations under the Emergency Powers (Defence) Act, 1940, notably under Essential Work Orders from 5 March 1941. By December 1944 Essential Work Orders covered 67,400 undertakings and 8,569,000 people (28 per cent women workers) (Parker, 1957, 499; Wrigley, 1996(b), 19–24).

After long negotiations, the Amalgamated Engineering Union (AEU) and the engineering employers came to an agreement over dilution, just six days before the outbreak of the war. This was supplemented by a second agreement on 11 September 1939 which was to cover the duration of the war. These agreements were also made much earlier in the war than their equivalents of the First World War and, moreover, they applied to all engineering work and not just government work.

The other big issues were pay and strikes. In the early part of the war there was substantial pressure on pay as unemployment fell and prices rose. However, from late 1940 until the end of the war the cost of living index stabilised, with the government subsidising costs and rationing limited supplies (Hancock and Gowing, 1949, 77, 166–70, 201 and 309).

As for strikes or lock-outs, Ernest Bevin used his special wartime powers to issue on 18 July 1940 the Conditions of Employment and National Arbitration Order (best known as Order 1305 as it was that number under Statutory Rules and Orders, 1940). Order 1305, which was replaced only in August 1951, made it illegal for employers or workers to take part in strikes or lock-outs (unless the dispute had been reported to the minister and after 21 days the minister had not referred the matter for settlement). Order 1305 was a supplement, not a replacement, of pre-war powers. During the war more than half of industrial disputes were resolved by the two parties negotiating. Of the rest, over 2000 settlements were reached under the auspices of conciliation officers of the Ministry of Labour under the Conciliation Act, 1896, 280 awards were made by the Industrial Court under the Industrial Courts Act, 1919, and some 2,200 were referred under Order 1305 to the National Arbitration Tribunal (or its Northern Ireland twin). Order 1305 reinforced collective bargaining as it required employers to recognise terms and conditions of employment agreed by bodies 'representative of substantial proportions of the employers and workers engaged in the trade or industry in the district in which the employer is engaged' (Wrigley, 1996(b), 26; Fishman, 1999).

The extension of collective bargaining was a major feature of the Second World War as it had been of the First World War. Again it was encouraged by the need for industry-wide agreements to facilitate wartime planning, with the government eager that the two sides of industry should resolve their own difficulties and differences. Where previously bargaining arrangements did not exist, as in the catering trade, Bevin was keen to introduce them, even when, as in the case of catering, it upset many Conservative MPs. In 1946, 46 of the 112 joint industrial councils or similar bodies which were active had been set up under Bevin (Bullock, 1967, 93).

At the apex of such arrangements were the national trade union and employer organisations. The TUC achieved near automatic access to ministers and senior civil servants on matters of major concern to trade unions (Martin, 1980, 277), though Bevin, like Lloyd George in the First World War, also used large union conferences not sponsored by the TUC to resolve particular problems in such industries as shipbuilding and building. Bevin was explicit that he was determined to back the trade unions, and this included bolstering trade union officials against militant members. Regulation IAA gave as an explicit aim (in the Ministry of Labour memorandum) that it was to 'strengthen the hands of the trades unions in dealing with irresponsible elements'.

From 22 June 1941, when Russia was in the war, communist activists in the trade unions usually worked hard to prevent strikes and to achieve high levels of output. The AEU, with Jack Tanner as its president in 1941, pressed hard for joint committees of employer and trade union representatives in all workplaces to boost production (Hinton, 1994). By late 1943 up to 60 per cent of engineering firms (with 60 or more workers) as well as the Royal Ordnance factories had such committees (Inman, 1957, 380–1; Croucher, 1982, 154–5). There were also district production committees in the coal industry (Court, 1951, 130–1, 210 and 318–23). Opposition to such moves came not from ministers such as Bevin or Lord Beaverbrook, both of whom were supportive, but from employers who feared that such committees would undermine managerial prerogatives.

However, in all probability most working people did not need such 'vanguard leadership' to respond to the needs of this war, given the enemy action on their factories and homes, the needs of British forces and the mass murder being committed in Nazi occupied territories. Yet, even so, the dissatisfactions and inefficiencies of some temporary labour should not be ignored (Mass Observation, 1943). Overall, as Broadberry and Howlett have concluded, when reviewing the very problematic data, it seems 'that output per employee did increase in many of the industries in the munitions and related sector between the production census years of 1935 and 1948' (Broadberry and Howlett, 1998, 58–60). They also cite Inman's example of where at one aircraft firm the number of workers per aircraft dropped from 487 to 220 between April 1942 and April 1943 (Inman, 1957, 204).

If the popular image of trade union unofficial dissent in the First World War is usually linked to militant engineers on Clydeside (1915–16) or elsewhere (notably May 1917), then that of the Second World War is linked to the miners. This is not surprising given that in 1940–4 the coal industry accounted for 46.6 per cent of all stoppages, 55.7 per cent of all working days lost through disputes and 58.5 per cent of all workers directly or indirectly involved in stoppages. Only two other sectors passed 5 per cent in any of these measurements of strikes: engineering (with 13.9 per cent of all stoppages, 18.9 per cent of working days lost and 18.0 per cent of workers involved) and shipbuilding (where the respective figures were 9.6, 9.3 and 6.2 per cent).

In the coal mines wartime grievances were added to a legacy of bitterness from 1919–26. An American report of 1944 commented on 'the bad feeling and antagonism which pervades the industry and which manifests itself in low morale, non co-operation and indifference'. During the war miners' wages were left behind by other workers in war-essential industries, especially so in South Wales, Scotland and the North-East. The most famous of several major disputes was at the Betteshanger colliery in Kent in 1941–2, where the Ministry of Mines arranged for summonses to be taken out against the 1,050 underground workers. When the miners were fined, and all but nine refused to pay, the government secured recommendations to the magistrates that no action should be taken. This illustration of the limitation of the law in wartime against determined collective action echoed the success of the South Wales miners in July 1915 (Supple, 1987, 25–34 and 569–77; Wrigley, 1996(b), 27–33).

The second most strike-prone sector was engineering. Here in 1941, there was serious unrest among young workers, who felt that employers were exploiting apprentices as cheap labour. There was also ample cause for dissatisfaction among women workers over discrimination in pay. One notable strike at Rolls Royce's Merlin engine works at Hellington, near Glasgow, in October–November 1943, was due to men receiving higher pay than women even though both were operating new, purpose-built simple machinery (Croucher, 1982, 285–92; Summerfield, 1984, 171–2).

Yet, if wartime industrial relations were not always as rosy as some myths would have it ('We all pulled together patriotically then, under Mr Churchill', or 'the workers broke production targets to help their comrades defend the Soviet Union'), generally the trade union movement emerged from the war with its size and its status in British politics and society enhanced.

Chapter 3

Trade union development, 1945–2000

The trade unions expanded until 1979, then contracted until 1998, after which there was a period of stabilisation (see Tables 3.1 and 3.2). From their early days, in the eighteenth century, onwards the trade unions' membership has changed as occupational groups have risen and fallen in size and significance in the economy. The trade unions' membership changed during their good years (1945–79) as well as afterwards (1980–2000). Both periods saw substantial trade union mergers, with the post 1979 period seeing large unions needing to merge in order to maintain their organisations and their services to members as the size of their memberships declined. In adverse conditions trade unions had to be more responsive to members' needs, to offer more and better services to secure their loyalty when the tangible benefits of trade union membership were less apparent but the dangers of being a trade union member were greater in a politically and economically hostile climate.

Trade union membership: expansion, 1946–79

British trade union membership reached its peak in 1979. Trade union membership rose from 8,603,000 in 1946 (the first full postwar year) to 12,639,000 in 1979. In terms of trade union density this was a rise from 43.0 per cent to 53.4 per cent, with male trade union density rising from 51.9 to 63.1 per cent and female trade union density from 24.3 to 39.4 per cent (Table 3.1).

The pace of trade union growth was uneven. While 1950–73 was the 'golden age' of the international economy, Britain benefited less than many of her competitors. Also British trade unions experienced the slowest growth rate of the 1945–79 period between

Table 3.1. *Trade union membership in Great Britain 1935–1985*

Year	Number of trade unionists (000s)	Percentage change over 5 years	Density (%)	Percentage change over 5 years
(a) Membership and density in five-year periods				
1935	4803[a]		25.1[a]	
1940	6519[a]	+35.7[a]	33.4[a]	+33.1[a]
1945	7684[a]	+17.9[a]	38.6[a]	+15.6[a]
1950	9003	+17.4[a]	44.3	+13.5[a]
1955	9460	+5.1	44.5	+0.5
1960	9437	−0.2	44.0	−1.1
1965	9715	+2.9	43.0	−2.3
1970	10672	+9.9	48.5	+12.8
1975	11561	+8.3	52.0	+7.2
1980	12239	+5.9	54.5	+4.8
1985	10282	−16.0	49.0	−10.1
(b) Female membership and density in five-year periods				
1935	738[b]		12.3[b]	
1940	1089[b]	+47.6[b]	17.6[b]	+43.1[b]
1945	1584	+45.6[b]	24.8[b]	+40.1[b]
1950	1650	+4.0[b]	24.0	+4.4[b]
1955	1827	+10.7	24.5	+2.1
1960	1879	+2.8	25.3	+3.3
1965	2099	+11.7	26.1	+3.2
1970	2583	+23.1	31.2	+19.5
1975	3263	+26.3	36.4	+16.7
1980	3771	+15.6	39.9	+9.6
1985	3470	−8.0	37.3	−6.5

Note: [a] These figures rest entirely on the Bain and Price data (Bain and Price, 1980, 40). The Waddington figures for the 1950–60 period only vary from these data by between 0.1 and 0.2 per cent, with the difference becoming greater thereafter, so the 1945–50 figures presented here should give a reasonable impression of the patterns of change. The Waddington data exclude the registered unemployed, employers, self-employed and members of the armed forces as well as retired and unemployed persons who retain trade union membership. Hence, for the analysis of union density, the union membership figures are lower than the Bain and Price figures in Table 3.1 (b). Also, from 1975, 31 organisations previously counted as trade unions were excluded from Department of Employment data (following the Trade Union and Labour Relations Act 1974).

Sources: Bain and Price (as above) and Waddington, 1992, 290.

[b] These figures rest entirely on the Bain and Price data (Bain and Price, 1980, 40). The Waddington figures only vary by up to 0.3 per cent from these data for 1950–60, with the difference becoming greater thereafter, so the 1945–50 figures presented here should give a reasonable impression of the pattern of change. Exclusions as for Table 3.2

Sources: Bain and Price, 1980, 40; Waddington, 1992, 293.

Table 3.2. *British trade union membership 1989–2001*

Year	Number of members (000s)	Percentage change in membership	Union density
1989	8939		39.0
1990	8835	−1.2	38.1
1991	8602	−2.6	37.5
1992	7956	−7.5	35.8
1993	7767	−2.4	35.1
1994	7530	−3.0	33.6
1995	7309	−2.9	32.1
1996	7244	−0.9	31.2
1997	7154	−1.2	30.2
1998	7155	0.0	29.6
1999	7277	1.7	29.5
2000	7351	1.0	29.4
2001	7295	−0.8	28.8

Source: Labour Force Surveys; *Labour Market Trends.*

1952 and 1968, only an average of 0.3 per cent, in spite of this being much of the main period of international economic boom. Trade union growth was greater during notably politically favourable periods and when high inflation encouraged hitherto weakly unionised sectors to unionise. There was steady growth of an average of 1.3 per cent per annum, 1946–52, during the Labour government of Clement Attlee (1945–51) and the period of post-war economic reconstruction. There was more rapid growth, an average of 2.7 per cent per annum, 1968–79, under the Labour governments of Harold Wilson (1964–70, 1974–76) and James Callaghan (1976–9) and the Conservative government of Edward Heath (1970–4), a period marked by high inflation and much government involvement in collective bargaining. Yet, while favourable political circumstances helped trade union growth in Britain, it should be recognised that trade union growth and decline were matched by similar developments in countries with governments of different political complexions.

Most explanations of trade union growth have rested on a mixture of economic factors combined with more particular ones such as government actions, employers' policies and changing industrial structures. Econometric studies of the relationship between the business cycle and the rate of change of trade union membership have pointed to the rates of change of retail prices and of wages as well as levels of unemployment as key economic determinants (Bain and Elsheikh, 1976, 26–70). During the period of fastest increases in trade union membership in Britain, the late 1960s and the 1970s, many hitherto lightly unionised groups of employees felt that they were being left behind in a period of very high inflation. After 1969 real wages increased slowly and in the late 1970s they declined. However, while this explanation is satisfactory for the 1968–79 period (and for 1915–19), it is not so good for 1950–2 and 1959–62, when there was marked inflation but not substantial accelerations in trade union growth. Bruce Western, in studying trade union growth between 1950 and 1990 in eighteen OECD countries, argued that trade unionism was strongest where it was helped by working-class parties holding office and favouring the trade unions, where centralised industrial negotiations enabled the trade unions to co-ordinate their efforts and where trade union management of welfare schemes enabled them to hold the loyalty of those in a weak market position (Western, 1997, 3). The UK was one country he classified as a country of middle trade union density (between high-density countries, such as the Scandinavian and low-density, such as the United States and Japan). Labour in office helped British trade unionism to grow, as did much national collective bargaining.

Trade union growth in Britain in 1945–79 took place in spite of adverse changes in industrial structure. There was a continuation of the decline of many of the old staple industries, a decline which had been very marked from 1921. In 1948 5.4 per cent of the civil labour force still worked in coal, cotton and man-made fibres and on the railways, but by 1971 these sectors occupied only 2.6 per cent of the labour force. These had been bastions of trade unionism, with densities of 86.4, 78.3 and 88.7 per cent respectively in 1948. By 1979 these densities were even higher, at 92.7, 87.6 and 96.8 per cent respectively, but by this time the overall numbers of workers in these sectors had declined; together, they had fallen from being 15.9 per cent of all trade unionists to only 4.6 per cent. There was a similar situation with the broad category of manual workers, where there was a 14.7 per cent fall in their overall numbers, while trade union density rose by 5.9 per cent between 1951 and 1979 (Wrigley, 1996c, 62–4).

While these areas of earlier trade union strength declined, they were superseded by growth elsewhere. Trade unionism expanded substantially in white-collar occupations as numbers employed grew rapidly. Between 1951 and 1979 white-collar workers grew from just under a third to a half of the British labour force. Between 1951 and 1968, even though white-collar trade unionism grew by 29.8 per cent, it did not keep pace with the growth of white-collar employment. However, between 1964 and 1970 white-collar trade unionism grew by 33.8 per cent, outstripping the growth of employment. By 1979 about 44 per cent of all white-collar workers were trade union members, and of all British trade unionists 40 per cent were white-collar workers (Bain and Price, 1980, 42).

George Bain in his classic study *The Growth of White-Collar Unionism* (1970) argued that particularly important explanations for growth were the degree of concentration of employment, the extent to which employers were willing to recognise trade unions representing white-collar employees and the extent to which government action promoted trade union recognition. Bain also suggested that white-collar workers joined unions, 'not so much to obtain economic benefits as to be able to control more effectively their work situation', as they felt they had less control over their jobs in the face of tighter bureaucratic controls (Bain, 1970, 183–88).

Jenkins and Sherman (1979) largely agreed with Bain but pointed to white-collar unions which had grown without national bargaining agreements and suggested his explanations tended 'to ignore the original growth in membership which has to precede recognition'. They also asked: 'why, after recognition, have some unions grown so much faster than others, given equal recruitment areas?' and: 'Why did ASSET [Association of Supervisory Staffs, Executives and Technicians], which had EEF [Engineering Employers' Federation] recognition in 1944, have to wait until the 1960s for its take-off?' (Jenkins and Sherman, 1979, 33).

One of the features of the growth of white-collar trade unionism was the very rapid growth of a few high-profile unions, notably ASSET, which in 1960–68 grew by 138.2 per cent, while aggregate British white-collar union membership rose by 20.7 per cent. The union had grown earlier under Tom Agar, a colourful figure, who had greatly expanded membership during the Second World War, secured the 1944 EEF recognition and had changed the name of the

National Foremen's Association to the wider aspirational name of ASSET (Melling, 2002). Dynamic and highly publicity-conscious leadership under Clive Jenkins from 1960 again played a major part in the growth of the union and its successor ASTMS (Association of Scientific, Technical and Managerial Staffs, 1968–88). Jenkins aimed for a very high profile in the TUC, Labour Party and the media. ASTMS became the fastest growing union in the TUC, increasing by 531 per cent from 1968 to 1974. Part of the rapid expansion was due to mergers, which have been categorised as aggressive (as opposed to defensive or consolidatory mergers) by Roger Undy and his colleagues in a major study of trade union development (Undy *et al.*, 1981, 203–14). Even without the mergers, the growth of ASSET and ASTMS was very rapid. Jenkins and his full-time union officials effectively built on strong support in engineering and developed a lesser volume of support in the aircraft and chemical sectors (Carter, 1986; Wrigley, 1999a). Jenkins' success was in a period of general trade union expansion, in which other white-collar unions also did well; the Clerical and Administrative Workers' Union growing, for example, by 34.3 per cent in 1960–8.

The later part of the 1945–79 period saw the beginnings of the catching up of unionisation among female employees. In industrialised countries other than Japan (which followed this trend from the mid 1970s) there was a substantial rise in the proportion of women of working age in paid labour, while there was a decline in the proportion of men of working age in employment. In the UK the number of paid female workers rose from 7.1 to 22.9 million, 1951–91. As a proportion women rose from 30.6 to 41.7 per cent of the labour force between 1956 and 1994. There was a very marked change in the composition of the female workforce. Before the Second World War most working women were under 30, whereas by the late twentieth century most were between 35 and 55. In 1960 20.2 per cent of mothers with children under school age worked, by 1991 this proportion had nearly tripled to 58.4 per cent (Walsh and Wrigley, 2001).

The trade unions very much needed to recruit more women. In 1945 two out of ten (20.6 per cent) British trade unionists were women. This rose to three out of ten (30.2 per cent) by 1979. There was also a notable rise in female trade union density over these years, from 24.8 to 40.4 per cent. Table 3.1 (b) shows the most rapid changes were after 1965. The percentage rise in the number of female trade unionists being 82.1 and in female trade union density being 13.8 over 1965–79 (Waddington and Whitston, 1995, 158). The trade unions have been condemned as patriarchal organisations antipathetic to female interests (Walby, 1986). One prominent feminist writer bluntly stated: 'I shall define patriarchy as a system of social structures in which men dominate, oppress and exploit women' (Walby, 1990, 20). In contrast Catherine Hakim has argued vigorously that the patterns of women employment, with the high levels of part-time work and occupational segregation, owed more to many women's preferences to prioritise family and domestic matters and to take up part-time work or homeworking while some, mostly professional, prioritise careers (Hakim, 1996). This view, in turn, aroused much controversy, with critics arguing that it had much truth in it, but was not a sufficient explanation of the different male and female employment patterns. Rosemary Crompton and others have argued that such individualist arguments neglect other aspects of the gender division of labour, such as structural constraints on women's opportunities. Work is based on male work patterns, not ones favourable to female priorities (Crompton, 1997, 16–19).

The needs of many women for differing work patterns were expressed at the time at TUC women's conferences and at other trade union conferences. For instance, in 1974, a delegate from the Society of Civil Servants said that:

> working conditions must be reorganized to recognise that the working life of most women will consist of periods of work interrupted, but not broken, by spells at home to bear and bring up their children . . . Very often a woman needs a period of part-time work, and flexi-hours are not the answer, because however late you arrive in the morning, you have got to stay late at night to make it up. Part-time work is really needed, but it is extremely difficult. The men do not like it . . . The employers do not like it; it is difficult to organise. On the other hand, if working women are able to continue their careers, organization of part-time work is absolutely essential.
>
> (TUC, *Report of TUC Women Workers' Conference 1974*, 82–3)

Many trade unions, especially in the three decades after the Second World War, acted contrary to the employment interests of women. Among early post-war examples of trade unions acting in such a way was the Union of Post Office Workers' 1953 conference which passed a motion calling on the union to press for the return of the marriage bar in the Post Office (i.e. women leaving employment on marriage), and, although this policy was revoked the next year, it was still applied to its own full-time officials until 1964 (Clinton, 1984, 432–3). Men often feared women would take the jobs available and undercut wage rates. There was also a more general failure of male-dominated unions to understand the needs of women, let alone to prioritise them. This was markedly so over many women's needs for flexibility in hours of work, better childcare arrangements and equal pay for equal work. Yet within the trade unions there were also liberal, democratic impulses which championed fair deals for female employees, not least by women trade union and trade council members.

In the economic good years up to 1979, most unions were slow to recruit part-time workers, four-fifths of whom were women. While the available statistics on part-time workers are none too reliable, especially in the earlier post-war period, they nevertheless clearly suggest a large expansion in numbers: from some 779,000 in 1951 to 3,781,000 in 1981. Many male trade unionists saw female part-time workers as a major threat, as cheap labour, and were hostile (Lewenhak, 1977, 267). In contrast, the TUC's Women's Advisory Committee, recognising many women's preference for part-time work, urged in 1966: 'While part-time women remain unorganized the committee believe they constitute a threat both to the effectiveness of the union machinery and to the security and working conditions of other workers.' Nevertheless, in spite of such arguments, until the 1980s the unions very clearly prioritised the concerns of their male members over the large number of female potential members.

Until at least the 1970s the trade unions were also very slow to act vigorously on their declared principles on equal pay. In 1952 the Labour-controlled London County Council made a beginning with teachers. Central government followed in 1954 when R. A. Butler, the Conservative Chancellor of the Exchequer, agreed to a six year phasing-in of equal pay in the civil service. This spread to other areas of the public sector, thereby helping these areas of employment hold on to their workforces in a period of labour shortage. In the private sector the Amalgamated Engineering Union (AEU) used its 'industrial muscle' in the mid 1950s to negotiate reductions in differentials. However, by 1959, women's average hourly pay was still only 77.4 per cent of that of men (Wrigley, 1999b, 53).

For too long most unions remained part of the problem, giving verbal support to equal pay but in negotiations not prioritising the issue. John Edmunds (later the General Secretary of the General Municipal Boilermakers and Allied Trades) and Giles Radice (later Labour MP) wrote in the Fabian Society pamphlet *Low Pay* (1968) that society 'broadly accepts that as women and juveniles have fewer financial responsibilities than men, it is tolerable that they should be paid less, irrespective of the value of the work'. They also observed that in pay bargaining 'there is a tendency for both these groups to be quietly put to one side and only considered after the "real" discussion (which, of course, concerns the pay of men) has been concluded'. They concluded: 'It is arguments like these which reinforce the case for some sort of guaranteed national minimum, set independently of collective bargaining.'

The national minimum wage, which still treated younger workers differently, came in 30 years later, but equal pay legislation was passed in 1970. This legislation followed a much-reported strike at Ford's car manufacturing plant at Dagenham, where Rose Boland, a shop steward, led striking sewing-machinists. As a result of intervention by Barbara Castle, Secretary of State for Employment and Productivity, the women received 92 per cent, not 85 per cent, of the men's rate of pay. She went on, with the Prime Minister's backing, to push forward what became the Equal Pay Act, 1970, which came fully into effect at the end of 1975. This had a substantial immediate effect, with UK women's average earnings as a percentage of men's rising in manufacturing from 47.0 to 58.1 for basic weekly wages, and from 54.1 to 66.2 for basic hourly wages (with the rise for all industries being from 53.7 to 64.3 and from 63.7 to 73.5 respectively) between 1970 and 1976. However, in other Western European economies there were similar reductions in the gender pay gap and in the late 1970s the gender pay gap remained bigger in the UK than in most other Western European countries (OECD, 1986). In 1998 the gender pay gap had only narrowed a little more, with women earning on average 75 per cent of the average male hourly wage. However, in part-time jobs the gender pay gap deteriorated in the late twentieth century (Desai *et al.*, 1999).

Female trade unionists repeatedly expressed other priorities as well as equal pay. In 1963 the TUC Women's Advisory Committee drew up an Industrial Charter for Women which listed, after equal pay, opportunities for promotion, apprenticeship schemes, better training for younger women and retraining for older women returning to work, and special provision for health, welfare and care. The Industrial Charter for Women was revised and expanded in 1968, 1975 and 1977. As with equal pay, some advance was made in the 1970s by legislation, with the Sex Discrimination Act, 1975, and the Employment Protection Act, 1975, which included provision for maternity leave. However, as with pay, the trade unions themselves were part of the problem facing women securing a better deal at work, with union pressure long weak in regard to improving women's employment conditions and work prospects (Rees, 1992, 84–107).

Trade union membership: contraction, 1980–2000

British trade union membership fell longer and further between 1979 and 1998 than even during the bad interwar years (see Table 3.1 and 3.2 above). In broad terms membership fell by around 40 per cent, though the basis of the figures changed in the late 1980s so a little caution needs to be exercised. Trade union density fell from about 53 to 30 per cent, 1979–98. The loss of overall trade union membership was halted in 1998 and small gains in membership occurred in 1999 and 2000, but not in 2001 (Table 3.2).

From 1989 there is more detailed information on the membership of British trade unions. This comes from Labour Force Surveys (LFS) which have asked a series of questions, the answers to which enable more detailed analysis. However, the level of union membership in these statistics is lower than the older source as the LFS data only cover those in employment in the week that the survey was taken. Earlier, the source of trade union membership statistics was the information that the trade unions provided the Certification Officer for Trade Unions and Employers' Associations. This information included members who were retired, unemployed or working overseas; all excluded from the LFS statistics.

The period from 1979 saw a continued contraction of employment in the old bastions of trade unionism. Trade unionism remained relatively strong in these areas, even after privatisation. In the production industries, mining and quarrying, manufacturing, electricity, gas and water supply, and also in transport and communications, there remained high rates of union density among male and manual workers. In 1999 union density among all employees in mining and quarrying was 37 per cent, in manufacturing 28 per cent, electricity, gas and water supply 52 per cent, transport and communications 42 per cent in contrast to such difficult to unionise areas as hotels and restaurants (6 per cent), agriculture, forestry and fishing (9 per cent) and real estate and business services (11 per cent).

The years of the Thatcher and Major governments (1979–97) were marked by a sharp decline in trade unionism in the private sector. Trade union decline was a feature of industrialised economies, reflecting in part more adverse international economic circumstances than in 1950–73 and a post-Keynesian hostility to trade unionism. In Britain the political climate was hostile to trade union membership, the law being tilted strongly against trade unions and, in the private sector in particular, many trade union activists being made redundant in the early 1980s. In 1999 only 19 per cent of employees in the private sector were in unions, in contrast to 60 per cent in the public sector. Trade unionism continued to be stronger in larger workplaces, with 26 per cent of employees in private sector workplaces of 25 or more employees being in unions while only 9 per cent were in smaller establishments (the public sector figures being 62 and 51 per cent).

The decline in employment and so of trade union membership of traditional supporters pushed the unions to address more the needs of women, workers from various 'ethnic' communities, young workers and those not working traditional hours. The new imperative with regard to women is well illustrated in the case of the print union, the Society of Graphical and Allied Trades (SOGAT). In 1968 the union set up a women's advisory committee to inform its executive committee, of whom 22 of 24 were men. After only five meetings, it was disbanded in 1972. In 1983 SOGAT's leadership, following the TUC's lead, took women's issues more seriously and set up a 'positive action committee' (Gennard and Bain, 1995, 487–8).

While the trade unions actively sought to recruit part-time work-ers, their attitude was more mixed concerning homeworkers. On the one hand, there was the view of the National Union of Hosiery and Knitwear Workers which in the late 1940s and the early 1970s had called for a common trade union response to homeworkers, fearing them as a source of cheap, non-union labour which could endanger factory jobs. On the other hand, there were others, no-tably at the TUC women's conferences, who sought not to prevent homeworkers earning a living but 'to ensure that they were pro-tected against exploitation and underpayment, bad working condi-tions and particularly against the risk of accidents'. They sought to bring homeworkers within the trade union movement.

In the 1980s and 1990s, as old-style factory employment crum-bled, homeworking remained widespread. It is difficult to be pre-cise as to how widespread, figures on homeworking being very sus-pect. One of the more credible assessments was made in 1971 in a Department of Employment research paper by A. Cragg and T. Dawson which estimated some 1.5 million (6 per cent of the labour force) worked at home. The Workplace Industrial Relations Surveys found that the percentage of employers who used homeworkers or outworkers as 8 per cent in 1980 and thereafter found the percent-age was around 4 or 5 per cent for the mid 1980s to the late 1990s (Millward *et al.*, 2000, 48). The attraction of homeworking to em-ployers was well put in a recent study: 'It is a form of produc-tion which can be grafted easily on to flexible manufacturing sys-tems and homeworkers are currently assembling, machining and packing products for some of the biggest companies in the world' (Rowbotham and Tate, 1998, 112).

In the late 1970s onwards the TUC and some trade unions ac-tively campaigned to secure better conditions of employment for homeworkers. Local surveys by several trades councils provided vivid evidence for such campaigns. At a time when the national press was full of stories of overmighty trade unions, such surveys revealing cases of very low pay, hazardous work practices (such as women soldering on kitchen stoves with infants present) and the use of unhealthy materials statutorily excluded from factories, pro-vided a reminder of why many working people in the past had felt a need for trade unions (Wrigley, 1999b, 49–50). Nevertheless, the trade unions continued to find those working at home very hard to recruit, the LFS figures for 1999 suggesting only 7 per cent were unionised.

The trade unions' record in seeking to recruit non-white workers was very mixed. For instance, a highly publicised strike at the Mansfield Hosiery Mills, Loughborough, in 1972 raised racial issues. Asian employees rarely progressed to more skilled jobs and the hosiery union was laggard in pressing for equality of opportunity (Wrigley, 1997, 157–9 and 187–8). Throughout the post-1945 period the trade union leadership was well aware of the potency of racist politics. When Edward Heath dismissed Enoch Powell from the Conservative Shadow Cabinet in April 1968 there were strikes in the London docks and in the West Midlands, with the strikers calling for free speech on race issues and often favouring the restriction of further immigration (Lindop, 2001).

However, as Ken Lunn has argued, the trade unions' attitude to race in the post Second World War period was not one dimensional (Lunn, 1999). While there was often hostility to the recruitment of non-British labour, there was frequent support within the labour movement for such workers, from Polish European Volunteer Workers at the time of the end of the Second World War to black and Asian workers later. In many areas trades council members and other trade union activists were prominent in the community relations councils which were formed from the late 1960s.

The TUC and several unions campaigned against racialism and for a multi-racial workforce from the mid 1970s onwards. The TUC has run annual Black Workers' Conferences since 1998. The April 1999 conference, held in Blackpool, was attended by 221 delegates plus representatives from 11 trades councils. At the September 2001 Congress, the TUC's affiliated trade unions each undertook a commitment 'to promote equality for all and to eliminate all forms of harassment, prejudice and unfair discrimination, both within its own structures and through all its activities, including its own employment practices'.

The trade unions after 1979 made greater efforts to unionise non-white workers as well as female workers. Union densities among black men and women were higher than among white workers by the mid 1990s. According to the LFS data, 42 per cent of black women and 39 per cent of black men were in unions compared to

29 per cent of white women and 35 per cent of white men (and 27 per cent of Indian women and 30 per cent of Indian men).

The TUC also sought to foster equality of treatment for disabled workers. It held a series of Disability Forums and after the 2000 Congress drew up a *Disability Action Plan* to serve as a guide to best practice for all its affiliated unions. It also became a major supporter of the Disability Rights Commission, formed in 2000, and its *Louder than Words* campaign. The TUC's first motions-based annual Disability Conference was held in 2001.

The fourth element in the TUC's drive for greater equality was on behalf of lesbian and gay workers. It set up a Lesbian and Gay Committee in 1998, with the aim to gain anti-discrimination legislation offering similar protection to that covering the grounds of sex and race by the Race Relations Act and Sex Discrimination Act. The first formal motions-based Lesbian and Gay Conference was held in 1998, the second in July 1999 was attended by delegates from 33 trade unions.

By the end of the twentieth century the number of female trade unionists was catching up the number of male. Also, by 1999 union density among women was 28 per cent compared with 31 per cent for men. Trade unionism was strongest in white-collar work, among public sector workers, in larger workplaces (with the exception of employees of banks and building societies) among full-time workers but with growing numbers of part-time workers. Trade union membership was more notable among those aged 30 and over and was weakest among those under 20. Trade union density was highest among those with A levels or equivalents (29 per cent), degrees or equivalents (37 per cent) or other higher education qualifications (44 per cent), whereas it was lowest among those whose highest qualification was GCSE or equivalent (22 per cent) or no qualifications (25 per cent). Most of the 1999–2000 increase in trade union membership came from recruiting part-time female workers. The most likely person to be a trade unionist was a female black in paid employment.

Trade unionism was strongest in 1999 in the North East of England (union density of 40 per cent), followed by Wales (39 per cent), Scotland (35 per cent), the North West of England (34 per cent), Yorkshire and the Humber (34 per cent), the West Midlands (31 per cent) and the East Midlands (30 per cent). It was weakest in the South East (22 per cent), the East (23 per cent), the South West (26 per cent) and London (27 per cent). According to LFS data, in 1999 some 8.5 million people, 36 per cent of employees, had their pay and conditions determined wholly or in part by collective bargaining.

Trade unions and mergers

Between 1945 and 2000 the number of trade unions fell from 781 to 221. Most of the reduction was due to amalgamations. There were two notable merger waves in the period, 1944–8 and 1966–87 (Waddington, 1995, 17–29).

The Second World War, like the First World War, provided an opportunity for some rethinking of trade union structures. The 1943 Congress asked the General Council of the TUC to review trade union structures, and before the end of the war reports had been sent by the TUC to the trade unions in many sectors of the economy. Change was facilitated by the Societies (Miscellaneous Provisions) Act, 1940. The three biggest mergers of the period resulted in the creation of the National Union of Mineworkers (NUM) on 1 January 1945, the reorganisation of the Institution of Professional Civil Servants (IPCS) involving 122 unions in 1945, and the Union of Shop, Distributive and Allied Workers (USDAW) on 1 January 1947.

Further amalgamations were made easier by the Trade Union (Amalgamations) Act, 1964. An Act in 1917 had required half the memberships to vote and for there to be a 20 per cent majority in favour of merger. This had not prevented many mergers. For instance, the Boilermakers' Society and the Shipwrights' Association both secured 64 per cent majorities to merge in 1963. But it did hamper some potential mergers. The 1964 Act required a simple majority of members in both unions or, alternatively, a union could, by a transfer of engagements, transfer its members to another union by a simple majority vote.

In 1971 the General Council of the TUC issued a circular urging its affiliated unions to consider mergers. The main advantages were considered to be 'a more rational structure of union organization and improved finances, the widening of the scope of recruitment and the removal of demarcation difficulties, increased efficiency of services to members and improved collective bargaining machinery'. The TUC's encouragement, along with the greater ease of carrying out mergers, provided a green light for ambitious trade union leaders.

The most substantial study of trade union development in the 1960s to the mid 1970s, by Undy *et al.*, divided trade union mergers into defensive, consolidatory and aggressive mergers. Their most notable example of a defensive merger was the creation of the Union of Construction, Allied Trades and Technicians (UCATT) in 1971 by unions which had lost 31 per cent of their membership since 1955, were in financial troubles and faced serious problems in the building trades. In the case of the Amalgamated Engineering Union (AEU) forming the Union of Engineering Workers (AUEW) in January 1971 it was very much a move by the AEU to consolidate its powerful position in the engineering industry (Undy *et al.*, 1981, 67–74 and 171–203).

Aggressive mergers, in the view of Undy *et al.*, were those where the major union involved was seeking substantial expansion, often into employment areas new to it. The Transport and General Workers' Union (TGWU) gained 60 per cent of its membership growth in 1970–5 by nine mergers. The largest of the TGWU's mergers were with unions in industries which already had substantial numbers of TGWU members. The expansion of the Association of Scientific, Technical and Managerial Staffs (ASTMS) owed a great deal to a series of mergers, and its greatest success in expansion was to go beyond its 1960s stronghold of engineering into banking, insurance and other areas in the 1970s (Undy *et al.*, 1981, 203–14; Wrigley, 1999a).

Jeremy Waddington's major analysis of trade union mergers emphasises that much of such activity has occurred in waves (1918–24 as well as 1944–8 and 1966–87 in the twentieth century), in contrast to the evolutionary character of the accounts of Pelling (1987) and others, or the work of Undy *et al.* (1981), or Clegg's reliance on the structure of collective bargaining to explain mergers. He ascribes importance to factors both external to the unions (notably relating them to long-term business cycles) and internal. He locates the development of mergers in the politics of bargaining, placing much importance on (i) the bargaining position of unions relative to employers and the state; (ii) the bargaining position of unions relative to competitor unions; and (iii) factional bargaining within the unions (Waddington, 1995, 4–5). His book sparked off a debate with Undy, who stressed continuities rather than waves and emphasised more the importance of union leaders' roles (Undy, 1996; Waddington, 1997).

Union mergers continued beyond the twentieth century. At the end of 1998 the ten largest unions, each with over 250,000 members, contained 69.9 per cent of trade union members, while the smallest 131 unions contained 1.0 per cent of members. The smaller unions, perhaps those up to 50,000 members (which in 1998 numbered 198 unions and contained 13.5 per cent of trade unionists), seemed liable to be involved in future mergers. Subsequently the banking unions merged in May 1999 to form UNIFI, the Institution of Professionals, Management and Specialists (IPMS) and the Engineers and Managers Association (EMA) merged in 2001 to form Prospect, and the merger of the Amalgamated Engineering and Electrical Union (AEEU) with the Manufacturing, Science and Finance Union (MSF) to form Amicus in 2002, made it the second largest trade union, overtaking the TGWU.

Trade Union finances and organisation

Often mergers have been necessary for trade unions to maintain strong organisations and to be able to provide effective services to members. Trade union finances were not always strong, even in the boom years.

For substantial periods trade union expenditure grew faster than trade union income. Trade union membership subscriptions lagged behind wages and prices between 1936 and 1950, while union expenditure rose faster (Roberts, 1956, 381–93). There was a period of financial stability during the affluent years of the 1950s to 1967, followed by a decline in their financial strength until 1981 (Willman *et al.*, 1993, 8–19; Latta, 1972). Willman *et al.* suggested that 'at 1989 prices unions were "worth" approximately £116.60 per member in 1967 – the post-war peak – and approximately £43.80 per member in 1979' (Willman *et al.*, 1993, 14). After 1979 the decline in trade union membership forced considerable financial and organisational changes on to the unions. After three decades of trade union subscriptions declining as a proportion of annual earnings, from 1979 they edged up: from 0.3 per cent in 1979 to 0.35 per cent in 1984 and 0.38 per cent in 1990. As John McIlroy has emphasised, this is low compared to the 1 per cent in Germany and higher proportions in Scandinavia (McIlroy, 1995, 44–5). From the Second World War onwards over half of trade union income was spent on working expenses. The proportion rose to 60 per cent in the 1960s, while between the late 1940s and 1970 the proportion of expenditure spent on provident benefits fell from about 31 to 21 per cent. In the 1980s and early 1990s total trade union income rose by 176 per cent, but inflation increased by 139 per cent and total expenditure rose by 200 per cent. The proportion of expenditure on working expenses rose from 74 per cent in 1979 to 88 per cent in 1995 (Kessler and Bayliss, 1998, 172–3).

The Second World War was marked by a reversal of interwar cuts in numbers of full-time officials. Clegg, Killick and Adams (1961) in their study of twelve trade unions provided figures on full-time officials, showing an increase from 476 in 1939, to 558 in 1945, 689 in 1951 and 709 in 1959, an increase of nearly 50 per cent over 20 years. The Ministry of Labour estimated that there were 1,661 trade union officers in 1933, 1,516 in 1939, 2,081 in 1945, 2,539 in 1951 and 2,534 in 1959. While this represented a two-thirds rise over 1939–59, in terms of members per officer, there was an estimated drop only from 1 to 3,996 to 1 to 3,792. This ratio improved somewhat with the fall in membership after 1979. In 1991 the mean was 3,229 members per official, much higher than the Western European norms of between 1,000 and 2,000 members per official (Kelly and Heery, 1994, 37–8).

Unions' financial controls have been deemed to have encouraged greater centralisation in the unions. With automated central subscription systems and specialist financial officers, branch and district committees have become more dependent on the centre (Willman *et al.*, 1993, 205).

The increasing proportions of female memberships highlighted the small number of female full-time trade union officials. In 1976 eleven substantial unions, each with a majority of female members, employed 420 male but only 30 female full-time officials and their delegations to the TUC were made up of 162 men and 30 women. Among these twelve unions were the National Union of Public Employees (NUPE), with a 65 per cent female membership and

120 male and 2 female full-time officials, and the Union of Shop, Distributive and Allied Workers (USDAW), with a 59 per cent female membership and 129 male and 4 female full-time officials (Hunt, 1982, 166).

This gross disequilibrium not surprisingly caused resentment. The most graphic illustration of this was the 1971 short-lived breakaway Women's Industrial Union, led by Pat Sturdy, a Lucas worker in Burnley, which had the effect of concentrating the minds of the members of the General and Municipal Workers' Union (GMWU) on the concerns of its female members (Boston, 1980, 294–5). NUPE responded to its own inequality for women by adopting quotas for its executive committee, reserving five additional places for women (with women eligible for all the other places as well). The TUC encouraged its affiliated unions to appoint more female delegates. At the 2000 Congress 76 unions sent 772 delegates, of whom 499 were male (64.6 per cent), 273 female (35.4 per cent), representing 4,147,089 affiliated male (61.5 per cent) and 2,598,818 female members (38.5 per cent). However, remedying the gender imbalance of full-time officials was carried out more slowly. The Kelly and Heery survey found in 1992 that 62 unions, employing 2,564 full-time officials, had but 302 female officials. They did find seven predominantly white-collar unions had women as a fifth or more of their officials (Kelly and Heery, 1994, 34–41).

Where women were employed as full-time officials there was a problem for them of their male colleagues viewing them as specialists to deal primarily with female members. While they were often the most eager and effective in organising women workers, including part-time workers, and responding to childcare and sexual harassment issues, they were not happy to be marginalised by male colleagues into dealing with only 'women's issues', a point well brought-out by Diane Watson in interviews in the mid 1980s (Heery and Kelly, 1988; Watson, 1988, 133–4). There were similar problems for the smaller number of non-white ethnic full-time officials.

With British trade unions employing less full-time officials per member than their West European counterparts, there was greater reliance on the voluntary or part-time work of their active members. These were the local trade union branch officials and, in many sectors of the economy, shop stewards (or those with different titles carrying out similar functions). Both groups carried out a variety of important and time-consuming jobs, which usually affected their leisure time. The price of such a role was often victimisation by employers, with large numbers of local branch officials and shop stewards being among the first to lose their jobs in the 1980s. This was in spite of shop stewards' often moderating role. A research paper by W. E. J. McCarthy, *The Role of Shop Stewards in British Industrial Relations*, for the Donovan Commission (1965–68) commented: 'For the most part the steward is viewed by others, and views himself as an accepted, reasonable and even moderating influence; more of a lubricant than an irritant' (McCarthy and Parker, 1968, 56).

A social survey carried out on behalf of the Donovan Commission found that shop stewards' functions varied substantially. Generally, they were then highly important in many unions for collecting in union subscriptions and being a major means of communication both ways between the union's headquarters and the members. More particularly, the Donovan Report (1968) summed up:

A minority of stewards do not negotiate with managers at all, whereas some of them negotiate over a wide range of issues. But over half of them regularly deal with managers over some aspect of pay, and about half of them deal regularly with some question relating to hours of work, the most common being the level and distribution of overtime. About a third of them regularly handle disciplinary issues on behalf of their members, and other matters which some of them settle include the distribution of work, the pace of work, the manning of machines, transfers from one job to another, the introduction of new machinery and jobs, taking on new labour and redundancy.

(Royal Commission, 1968, 26)

At the time of the Donovan Report it was estimated that there were some 175,000 shop stewards and some 3,000 full-time trade union officials (McCarthy and Parker, 1968). With trade union strength growing and with more decentralised bargaining, the numbers of shop stewards grew. The cause of shop steward representation was also assisted in 1971 when the Commission on Industrial Relations published a report on facilities for shop stewards which recommended that there should be formalisation of their role, based on collective agreements made by employers and unions. Shop steward organisation spread from manufacturing into distribution, the service industries, local government, the National Health Service and elsewhere. By 1979 estimates put the number of shop stewards and other workplace representatives at 350,000, with this being common for manual workers. With the decline in employment and trade union membership in manufacturing industry and hostile trade union legislation, there was a marked decline in numbers from 1984 (McIlroy, 1995, 40–2).

When trade unionism shrank, there remained substantial workplace representation, especially in the private sector. These representatives were consulted by management but were rarely involved in collective bargaining. The significance of such work groups was noted by the Donovan Commission: 'Work groups can exert considerable control over their members even where there are no trade unions, or where trade unions refuse them recognition.' In 1980 the Workplace Industrial Relations Survey found union representation present in 53 per cent and non-union representation in 16 per cent of workplaces (but with a further 12 per cent with representation of unknown status), whereas in 1998 the union representation had fallen to 33 per cent and the non-union representation had risen to 41 per cent of all workplaces (Terry, 1999; Millward *et al.*, 2000, 115).

The tougher times of the 1980s and 1990s forced the trade unions to reassess the main functions of the unions and how to ensure they were carried out most effectively. Writers such as Willman, Morris and Aston (1993) have emphasised a view of the trade unions as 'labour-intensive service businesses'. John McIlroy has been critical of too much emphasis on assessing trade unions' success by financial objectives, instead stressing the importance in recruitment of 'the assertion of the primacy of trade unionism as a social and political movement' (McIlroy, 1997, 107–9).

Services to members became part of the trade union movement's strategies to hold on to members and to recruit more. By the end of the century trade unions were offering a considerable number of financial and legal services, including credit cards, conveyancing and life insurance. More important for convincing members of the benefits of staying have been representation at employment tribunals and helpline advice. In 1999, trade union support for members going to seek redress of grievances before employment tribunals helped secure £14.3 million, often with settlements made before

cases reached a tribunal. According to the TUC, unions helped secure wins or compromises in 92 per cent of the cases they took up.
Union helplines proved popular. In 1999, 22 unions ran 45 helplines
taking over 180,000 calls, which were often over legal issues, stress
and bullying at work. Such services which were integral to the main
roles of unions, along with the campaigns targeted at women, young
workers, ethnic groups and part-time workers, played a part in the
deceleration of trade union membership losses and the stabilisation
of membership at the end of the century.

Chapter 4

Strikes 1945–2000

Strikes feature prominently in almost any list of what was wrong with British industrial relations or British trade unionism after 1945. Strikes, especially unofficial strikes, were deemed to be a feature of 'the British disease'. The Royal Commission on Trade Unions and Employers' Associations 1965–1968, chaired by Lord Donovan, was much concerned about the increasing 'resort to unofficial and unconstitutional strikes and other forms of workshop pressure' (Royal Commission, 1968, 261).

Such concerns have led to a considerable literature discussing the nature of strikes in Britain. What were the main causes? Were some industries, some industrial plants, even some particular parts of plants more strike prone than others? Were strikes in some way uniquely a British problem? Was the pattern changed during the Thatcher years (1979–90) or Thatcher–Major years (1979–97)? These are some of the questions which have arisen on a topic which has been a major component of popular conceptions, or misconceptions, of 'overmighty trade unions'.

The statistics on strikes after the Second World War are relatively good. As ever, there remain relatively minor problems of comprehensiveness. Apart from the matter of whether small, short strikes have been reported at all, even those which have been reported have not been included in the statistics if they have lasted less than a day and involved fewer than ten workers unless 100 or more working days have been lost.

The bigger issue is which series of statistics to use. Those on numbers of strikes provide an indicator of how widespread strikes were, but do not discriminate between national strikes involving large numbers of people over weeks from brief local stoppages involving a few people. Statistics on the numbers of strikers involved give a better idea of the scale of disputes but not as to the duration of disputes. On the whole, statistics on the numbers of working days lost through strikes are preferable, as they provide an indication of the likely economic cost of disputes; but such figures on their own lose the dimension of the extensiveness of strikes (as one lengthy large national strike can result in as many working days lost as, in another year, a multitude of small disputes).

The broad pattern of strikes, 1945–2000

After the Second World War all the strike measurements broadly fell until 1951 but did not rise above 1945 levels in numbers of strikes or total working days lost until 1955. In 1945–51 the trade union movement was strongly supportive of the first majority Labour government (1945–51) in its struggle to reconstruct the British economy. The wartime prohibition on striking, Order 1305, was only removed in August 1951. There was also a sense of foreboding, based on knowledge of recessions after the Napoleonic, Boer and First World wars. James Cronin has commented of the period up to the 1960s: 'During the early postwar period of full employment, workers seem to have continued to operate within a depression mentality' (Cronin, 1979, 138).

From 1953 onwards there was a return of major national, official strikes, beginning with a one-day engineering strike in 1953. It was followed by big strikes involving railway workers, dockers, busmen and printers. The previous industry-wide strike had been in textiles in 1933. The 1950s also saw the growth of shop-floor representation, which appears to have encouraged trade union leaders to press harder for better pay and working conditions. In engineering there was a considerable growth in the numbers of unofficial strikes. The strike wave of 1957–62 was marked by small unofficial strikes and reflected insecurities linked to inflation, redundancies and the 'stop-go' British economic climate (Cronin, 1979, 139–40; Gilbert, 1996a, 137 and 142).

There was another strike wave, 1968–74. This followed on from slowly rising or stagnating real wages, 1964–8, under another majority Labour government (1964–70). After much restraint, there was an upsurge in strike action when substantial price rises occurred after the devaluation of the pound sterling in 1967. The failed attempt by the Labour government in 1969 to legislate for better industrial relations (with its White Paper, *In Place of Strife*, 1969 (Cmnd. 3888), indicating its intentions) and the introduction of the Industrial Relations Act, 1971, by the Conservative government (1970–4) politicised strikes. As well as some wage-claim strikes being aimed at the government as the employer of public sector workers, there were sixteen substantial strikes of political protest, involving some 6 million workers and the loss of some 6 million working days, 1969–73 (Durcan *et al.*, 1983, 170 and 438).

The unrest lessened with another Labour government taking office in 1974, which repealed the Industrial Relations Act, 1971, steadily reduced inflation and provided much by way of 'the social wage' (notably social welfare and housing improvements) and a reduction in income tax. However, the incomes policy again undercut real wages and led to a further rise in strike activity, 1977–9, ending in early 1979 with the 'winter of discontent', marked by low paid public sector workers, road haulage and others striking.

Levels of strike activity dropped in the 1980s and fell even further in the 1990s. In the 1990s the average number of working days lost due to strikes was 660,000, compared with 7.2 million in the 1980s and 12.9 million in the 1970s. The 1980s statistics are dominated by two huge strikes, both attempting to resist government policy to reduce employment substantially. These were in steel, in 1980, and in the coal industry, 1984–5. Together they contributed a third of all working days lost, 1980–9. The 1980s and 1990s were also marked by a substantial decline in the number of strikes and the numbers of working days lost in the private sector of the economy. The twentieth century ended with 1997 having the lowest ever recorded number of working days lost through strikes (records beginning in 1893) and 1999 having the second lowest (see Table 4.1).

Causes of strikes

While there are ample statistics on causes of strikes, these have not been very dependable as the causes of many strikes have often been complex and deep-rooted. The statistics have usually focused on 'the principal cause' of a strike. Often strikes have had multiple causes, with those on strike sometimes having different views as

Table 4.1. *Industrial disputes in the UK, 1945–2001*

Year	No of disputes	No. of workers involved (000s)	Total working days lost (000s)
1945	2293	531	2835
1946	2205	526	2158
1947	1721	620	2433
1948	1759	424	1944
1949	1426	433	1807
1950	1339	302	1389
1951	1719	379	1694
1952	1714	415	1792
1953	1746	1370	2184
1954	1989	448	2457
1955	2419	659	3781
1956	2648	507	2083
1957	2859	1356	8412
1958	2629	523	3462
1959	2093	645	5270
1960	2832	814	3024
1961	2686	771	3046
1962	2449	4420	5798
1963	2068	590	1755
1964	2524	872	2277
1965	2354	868	2925
1966	1937	530	2398
1967	2116	731	2787
1968	2378	2255	4690
1969	3116	1654	6846
1970	3906	1793	10980
1971	2228	1171	13551
1972	2497	1722	23909
1973	2873	1513	7197
1974	2922	1622	14750
1975	2282	789	6012
1976	2016	666	3284
1977	2703	1155	10142
1978	2471	1003	9405
1979	2125	4608	29474
1980	1348	834	11964
1981	1344	1513	4266
1982	1538	2103	5313

Table 4.1. (*cont.*)

Year	No of disputes	No. of workers involved (000s)	Total working days lost (000s)
1983	1364	574	3754
1984	1221	1464	27135
1985	903	791	6402
1986	1074	720	1920
1987	1016	887	3546
1988	781	790	3702
1989	701	727	4128
1990	630	298	1903
1991	369	176	761
1992	253	148	528
1993	211	385	649
1994	205	107	278
1995	235	174	415
1996	244	364	1303
1997	216	130	235
1998	166	93	282
1999	205	141	242
2000	212	183	499
2001	194	180	525

Sources: Ministry of Labour Gazette; Employment and Productivity Gazette; Department of Employment Gazette and Labour Market Trends.

to why they have gone on strike, and so emphasis on a principal cause overlooks much. There is also often a powerful 'straw that broke the camel's back' aspect to many strikes. While the prime and immediate cause may be a wage demand, often behind such an issue can be a substantial mixture of dissatisfaction. Such discontent can include such matters as resentment at working too long hours (including expectations of working long hours of paid overtime), poor working conditions, unreasonable foremen or supervisors and boredom of repetitive work.

Yet, in spite of such substantial drawbacks, a broad picture of the causes of strikes has emerged from various scholars' researches. For the period 1966–73 Durcan *et al.* found that the main immediate causes of strikes were wage increase claims and other wage issues, workplace discipline, redundancy, sympathy, demarcation conflicts and trade union principles (Durcan *et al.*, 1983, 437).

Table 4.2. *Working days lost through strikes over wages 1946–2001*

Year	(average) Percentage	Year	(average) Percentage
1946–52	44.6	1980–83	68.5
1953–57	82.0	1986–89	69.4
1960–68	66.5	1990–92	50.2
1969–73	84.6	1993–96	58.2
1974–79	85.1	1997–2001	57.2

Sources: Durcan *et al.*, 1983, 36, 66, 102 and 141; Walsh, 1983, 134; Kessler and Bayliss, 1998, 245; and *Labour Market Trends*.

By far the biggest cause of strikes has been wage issues. The numbers of strikes attributed to wage issues has varied more from year to year than non-wage causes of strikes. Strikes ascribed to wage issues reached high levels in 1955–8, 1960–1, 1964, 1968–74 and 1977–80. Until the 1970s a marked feature of these peak years of strikes over wages was that they were years when there were national engineering stoppages. As well as the engineering and metals sectors, those with the highest proportions of strikes which were deemed primarily over wages were shipbuilding, textiles and vehicle manufacturing (Durcan *et al.*, 1983, 143 and 181–3). Overall, wage issues were deemed to be the principal cause of around 44–48 per cent of strikes between the Second World War and 1968, but from 1969 to 1979 this percentage jumped up to an average of 57 per cent. It dropped back markedly to 38 per cent on average, 1981–95. From 1957 there are statistics for the numbers of working days lost through strikes for various causes. These reinforce this view of the relative importance of wage issues in strikes (see Table 4.2).

While the wage issues were mostly raised by the employees, many of the non-wage issues leading to strikes were raised by employers. This is so with such issues as discipline, manning levels and redundancy, but not with demands for shorter hours and perhaps not with many disputes over trade union principles. In 1946–59 strikes over trade union principles were substantial, ascribed as the primary cause of between 21 and 23 per cent of strikes. Yet, while remaining a substantial non-wage attributed cause of strikes, this cause fell markedly after 1959: from 10.5 per cent in 1960–8 to

6.8 per cent in 1969–73 and to 3.3 per cent in 1974–81. The probable reason for this decline in strikes over trade union principles is that trade union organisation became more widely established in the 1960s and 1970s. In the 1950s part of the explanation of these high proportions of strikes lies in struggles to secure shop floor representation. In contrast, the harsher political climate for trade unions, reinforcing the harsher economic climate, saw a sharp rise in struggles over redundancy issues after 1979.

The massive 1984–5 coal-mining dispute, which lost 26 million working days, marked the end of coal mining being a major feature in strike statistics. As James Cronin has commented of miners before then: 'What has distinguished miners more sharply from other workers has not . . . been a higher level of activity during eras of general conflict, but the ability to sustain militancy when others cannot.' There were large numbers of mining strikes during 1927–56, years when industrial relations in other sectors were generally relatively peaceful (Cronin, 1979, 162). In 1956 and 1957 about 80 per cent of strikes were in the coal industry, a myriad of short, sharp local disputes (2,076 in 1956, 2,224 in 1957). Between 1946 and 1973 there were 186 major stoppages (5,000 days or more) in the coal industry, with national stoppages in 1948, 1969 and 1972. The causes of unrest were complex, including resentments at past defeats, notably in 1926, but mostly primarily linked to wage issues and, after 1957, concern about redundancies as the industry was reduced in size; though with the National Power Loading Agreement, 1966, there was a reduction in small strikes (Durcan *et al.*, 1983, 240–7 and 267–71; Ashworth, 1985).

Strike-proneness

A major feature of strikes is that they were not spread evenly across the country, across industries or even within large industrial plants. Some areas of Britain have experienced more strikes than others, as have some industries, such as (at various times) coal, docks and cars. The prevalence of strike-prone industries in some regions obviously affect the regional strike characteristics, but then there are notable differences within industries from region to region.

There has been interest in the geographic spread of strikes from soon after the collection of strike statistics began. The *Labour*

Gazette, June 1893, provided a map of the distribution of strikes in 1891. The issue was discussed later in greater depth by K. G. J. C. Knowles (Knowles, 1952, 185–209) who measured strike-proneness by dividing the percentage of strikers in a region by the percentage of the industrial population (the UK as a whole being 1.0, having 100 per cent of both strikers and industrial population). He found for 1911–June 1945 that the regions or countries that on average were more strike-prone were South Wales (4.8), the West Riding of Yorkshire (2.4), Lancashire and Cheshire (2.0) and Scotland (1.1). Knowles also estimated regional/national strike proneness after statistically eliminating the effects of preponderances of strike-prone industries in areas (for instance, eliminating the effect of large numbers of miners in South Wales). When this was done his standardised regional/national list placed South Wales (1.3), West Riding of Yorkshire (1.2), Northern Ireland (1.2), Lancashire and Cheshire (1.1), and Scotland (1.1) all above average with all other areas well below average (1.0). Knowles observed that regional strike-proneness was partially conditioned by:

> certain sociological factors, rooted perhaps deeper in the region than the industries themselves. These may, for example, affect the size of firms, they may produce communities of a different kind from those of workers in the same industries who live in other regions; and they may thus influence the workers' attitudes to striking.
>
> (Knowles, 1952, 193)

However, overall, Knowles argued that 'regional differences... prove much slighter than industrial' and 'regional influences on striking are to a large extent industrial causes in disguise' (Knowles, 1952, 208–9). Knowles found that the workers most prone to strike in 1911–June 1945 were those in mining (6.7), textiles (4.3), metals, engineering and shipbuilding (1.3) and transport (1.1). He also analysed strike-proneness *within* industries. In the case of coal, South Wales (2.1) and the West Riding of Yorkshire (2.0) were well above average, with Scotland average (1.0). In metals, engineering and shipbuilding, the most strike-prone areas were Northern Ireland (6.8), much affected by huge disputes in 1919 and 1944, South Wales (2.2), Scotland (1.8), Northumberland and Durham (1.3) and Lancashire and Cheshire (1.2).

More recent writers (Smith *et al.*, 1978; Beaumont and Harris, 1988; and Gilbert, 1996a and c) have followed Knowles in putting much emphasis on geographic dimensions of proneness to strike. David Gilbert has emphasised two major aspects of the geography of strikes. One is the development of new industries, and that the development of this group of industries, 'away from older heartlands of union organisation, militancy and established industrial communities, has led to relatively low levels of strike activity'. The second is that 'the history of strikes also exhibits some degree of... "regional resilience"' (Gilbert, 1996a, 151).

The motor-car manufacturing industry provides some notable examples of the variety of features of strike proneness. According to Durcan, McCarthy and Redman's (1983) work on strikes between 1946 and 1973, 48 per cent of those in motor manufacturing occurred in the West Midlands, 21 per cent in the South East, 12 per cent in the North West and 7 per cent in Scotland. Within a company, such as Ford, there were major variations in strike levels between plants. When the Macmillan government (1957–63) successfully put pressure on the major companies to locate their additional plant in areas of high unemployment, this included going into places with a tradition of strikes, as was the case with the Ford plant at Halewood on Merseyside.

Yet, nevertheless, other commentators have put more emphasis on company policy and on problems specific to individual plants. Turner and his colleagues observed that, while some car-manufacturing plants which were isolated from others, such as Vauxhall at Luton, enjoyed relatively tranquil labour relations, in Coventry there was a mix of experiences,

the Rootes plant seemed unaffected by the Standard strikes of the mid 1950s, and Standard appears to have been quite uninvolved by the Rootes movement of 1959–60 – while neither of these groups, in their quite long intervals of relative quiescence, responded to the chronic militancy of Jaguar's workers.

(Turner *et al.*, 1987, 349)

The theme of strike-prone plants, or even parts of plants, is a recurring one in studies of post-1945 strikes (e.g., Prais, 1978). A detailed analysis of strikes in the turbulent period 1971–3, undertaken on behalf of the Department of Employment, found that even then 'only five per cent of plants experienced stoppages and of those over two-thirds had only one stoppage'. Within this 5 per cent there was a strike-prone minority: 5 per cent of these 'accounted for a quarter of stoppages and two-thirds of days lost in manufacturing'. There was a 'robust relationship' between strike incidence and larger plants. This led to the authors' conclusion: 'It is abundantly clear that Britain does not have a widespread strike problem but rather a problem of stoppages concentrated in a small minority of manufacturing plants and in certain non-manufacturing sectors' (Smith *et al*., 1978, 86–7 and 63).

Strikes: a British disease?

During the 1960s the notion that Britain suffered from endemic strikes became widespread. It was a view which became a norm in much of the popular press, in political argument and in much entertainment. Poor British industrial relations were memorably portrayed in the films *I'm All Right Jack* (1959), *The Angry Silence* (1960) and even *Carry On Cabby* (1963) as well as on television, most notably in London Weekend Television's comedy, *The Rag Trade*, with Miriam Karlin playing a strike-happy shop-steward who endlessly called: 'Everyone out'.

However, throughout the post-Second World War period such views have been countered by considering British industrial relations in a wider context. One of the earliest academic debates concerning strikes in this period was over Ross's and Hartman's argument that, in Western industrial societies, 'the strike has been going out of style' and 'withering away' (Ross and Hartman, 1960). This was an unfortunate assessment, given what followed in the next two decades. It was based on international comparisons of strike statistics for 1948–56 with 1900–29 and 1930–47, and was criticised for its handling of the statistics and for over-simplification (Ingham, 1974, 12–23). Nevertheless, it put strikes in an international setting.

When the Royal Commission on trade unions and employers organisations (1965–8), chaired by Lord Donovan, took up the issue of whether Britain was peculiarly strike-prone, it did so by international comparisons. The Donovan Commission drew on International Labour Organisation (ILO) statistics to analyse stoppages in major sectors (mining, manufacturing, construction and transport) by working days lost per involved worker. The outcome was that the Donovan Report (1968) put Britain in an intermediate group of countries between those with the least strikes, which included France and Japan, and those with a notably worse record, which included Australia, Canada, the United States, Ireland and Italy.

The Donovan Report's comparative assessment led to a debate which focused on the statistical problems of making international comparisons. H. A. Turner in *Is Britain Really Strike-Prone?* (1969) raised questions of differing definitions of 'a strike' (including when is a strike *one* strike) and of the effectiveness of the reporting of strikes in different countries, and argued that other countries would have more strikes recorded if they included stoppages on the same basis as was done in the British statistics. W. E. J. McCarthy rejected this view of the statistics, writing that it was arguable that Britain used a more restrictive definition than other countries (McCarthy, 1970). This led to further analysis of the extensiveness of strikes not recorded in British statistics (involving stoppages of less than a day and under ten workers). W. A. Brown's research suggested that the under-recording of working days lost by strike action amounted to about 6 per cent (Brown, 1981).

All this re-emphasises the need to be very cautious about comparative international statistics. However, when such concerns are recognised, there still remains a broad pattern over time which undermines the notion that proneness to strike was a peculiarly British disease of the 1960s and 1970s. Table 4.3 presents comparative figures for the periods 1961–9, 1970–9 and 1980–9 for working days lost per thousand workers in mining, manufacturing, construction, and transport and communication, with a fourth column giving the 1980–9 figures for all industries (not available for the earlier years). Table 4.4 provides figures for 1946–50 and 1957–91 in five year averages, again for the same major sectors (Wrigley, 1997, 25).

From such comparisons it appears that Britain's relative position remained broadly the same. Where there was a deterioration was in the late 1960s and early 1970s, but this was not relatively great enough to push Britain to the top of the league of strike-prone countries as most countries experienced an upsurge of strikes in that period (Coates and Topham, 1986, 213).

Similarly, there was no dramatic transformation during the years of Mrs Thatcher's governments. Kessler and Bayliss observed of the

Table 4.3. *Working days lost per 1,000 workers in ten countries 1961–1989 (mining, manufacturing, construction, and transport and communication; rank order in brackets; fourth column gives all industries and services)*

| | Annual Averages | | | All industries |
	1961–1969	1970–1979	1980–1989	1980–1989
Australia	424 (5)	1298 (3)	770 (2)	350 (4)
Canada	1026 (3)	1840 (1)	960 (1)	470 (2)
France	321 (6)	312 (7)	150	80
Germany (West)	24	92	50	50
Ireland	1114 (2)	1163 (5)	530 (4)	380 (3)
Italy	1438 (1)	1778 (2)	290 (7)	620 (1)
Japan	239	215	20	10
Sweden	18	42	330 ($=5$)	180 (6)
United Kingdom	274 (7)	1088 (6)	740 (3)	330 (5)
United States	1001 (4)	1211 (4)	330 ($=5$)	120 (7)

Source: Employment Gazette, December 1971, October 1973, January 1981 and December 1991.
Note: From the mid 1980s the French figures have a significantly different coverage. Also, the series for France does not include 1968.

British strike record in the 1980s that 'the reductions in the UK's incidence were not larger than those of its main competitors, nor did they bring it anywhere near the extremely low incidence in Germany and the Netherlands' (Kessler and Bayliss, 1998, 214). Nor was this due only to Thatcherite determination to enforce change in the steel and coal industries, for Britain's rank order remained unchanged in 1985–9. For all the trade union legislation of 1980–93 Britain did not become a strike-free zone as some predicted, although there was a substantial drop in strike activity in the 1990s, but perhaps still not the 'withering away' heralded by Ross and Hartman (Bassett, 1986).

The overall picture of the British strike level is that it has risen and fallen along with the broad movements of strikes in the other major industrial economies. The more detailed pattern has been affected by national political, economic and industrial circumstances. With even major changes in national economic policies, these have not occurred in isolation, but in response in large part at least to

Table 4.4. *Working days lost per 1,000 workers in nine countries in five-year periods, 1946-1991 (mining, manufacturing, construction, and transport and communication)*

	1946–1950	1957–1961	1962–1966	1967–1971	1972–1976	1977–1981	1982–1986	1987–1991
Australia	1292	306	358	796	1490	1250	630	544
Canada	1088	596	768	1682	2198	1562	944	770
France	1537	288	322	313	338	230	148	82
Germany (West)		26	34	80	32	86	100	6
Italy		676	1388	1692	1996	1508	612	414
Netherlands	200	61	16	42	82	80	30	40
Sweden	36	10	26	62	18	470	8	174
United Kingdom	148	352	228	608	968	1120	976	236
United States	2458	1166	790	1644	1054	900	316	206

Sources: International Labour Office Year Book, Ministry of Labour Gazette, Employment Gazette.
Note: Figures show five-year average, not weighted for employment. The series for France does not include 1968.

changed international economic circumstances. Hence, changes in the international economy have often impacted not only on levels of strike activity but also more generally on the fortunes of organised labour (Wrigley, 2000).

Strike ballots and industrial action

Before 1984 many trade unions held pre-strike ballots, in line with their rule books. Many did not. The Trade Union Act, 1984 made such ballots obligatory, otherwise trade unions calling strikes without such democratic endorsements lost their legal immunities for breaches of contracts. The TUC opposed this measure, but it was probably one of the few truly popular elements with trade union members of the Conservative legislation of 1980–93.

At first, in 1987–9, the 1,103 pre-strike ballots were only occurring before a small proportion of strikes. By 1990 the Advisory, Conciliation and Arbitration Service (ACAS) was reporting that such ballots were universal, while by 1992 a survey of the eighteen largest unions suggested that twice as many ballots were held as strikes occurred, even though most ballots went in favour of strike action (Dickens and Hall, 1995, 282). What happened was that trade union negotiators soon realised that strike ballots could be used to increase pressure on employers to make further concessions (Elgar and Simpson, 1993, 102–5). The proportion of those supporting strike action averaged over 90 per cent in 1987–9 and 1995, according to ACAS (Hanson, 1991, 54; Kessler and Bayliss, 1998, 255).

In 2000 the UK had the tenth lowest strike rate among the 23 OECD countries. In 2000 the numbers of days per thousand employees in the UK were 10, compared to 16 in the USA, 38 in Denmark, 62 in Italy, 72 in France, 88 in Australia, 139 in Spain, 168 in Ireland and 190 in Canada. Apart from 1996, since 1990 the UK strike rate has been lower than the average for either the OECD or the EEC. A feature of union ballots in 2000–1 was that nearly two-thirds of the 690 ballots (excluding 1,236 ballots over one issue) were for action short of a strike. In these ballots and strike ballots there was overwhelming support for the unions from their members; 91 per cent support for action short of a strike and 81 per cent support for strikes. In 2000, the main causes of disputes (multiple causes resulting in over 100 per cent totals) leading to ballots were pay (44 per cent), changes to working practices, including hours of work (29 per cent), working conditions (29 per cent) and trade union issues, including recognition (15 per cent). In 2001 such ballots were dominated by pay issues (72 per cent), with changes to working practices (25 per cent) being the major other cause. Nearly all action in 2000 was official (94 per cent), with 72 per cent backing pay claims, 46 per cent banning overtime and 40 per cent supporting one-day strikes. The unions won all or part of their demands in 76 per cent of the cases where there had been positive responses in ballots (TUC, 2001).

Chapter 5

Incomes policies, 1948–1979

In the post-Second World War years low levels of unemployment and relatively high levels of economic growth in a rapidly expanding international economy put organised labour in a strong position in the British labour market. By the mid 1950s inflation had replaced unemployment as the prime concern of many Conservative politicians. For three decades voluntary or statutory incomes policies were one of the major responses to wage inflation by British governments. Such statutory policies ran counter to trade unionists' deeply held belief in free collective bargaining.

For many years incomes policies were a highly contentious area between governments and the trade union movement. Before discussing the controversies over the effectiveness or ineffectiveness of such policies, it is best to outline the key features of these policies between 1948 and 1979.

The incomes policies, 1948–1979

Clement Attlee's Labour government (1945–51), struggling to reconstruct the British economy after the Second World War, called for voluntary restraint on wage rises in 1948. Attlee, in a statement in the House of Commons on 4 February 1948, declared that it was 'essential that there should be the strictest adherence to the terms of collective agreements', that in the current circumstances there was 'no justification for any *general* increase of individual money incomes' and that any wage or salary claim 'must be considered on its national merits and not on the basis of maintaining a former relativity between different occupations and industries'. This prime ministerial statement was followed by the 1948 White Paper,

Statement on Personal Incomes, Costs and Prices (Cmd. 7321). The trade union leadership was concerned about such a policy but was willing to support a Labour government in times of economic adversity to achieve 'general stabilisation' but called for the government 'not only to stabilise but to reduce profits and prices'. The 1948 TUC endorsed this support for the White Paper overwhelmingly (73 per cent for, 27 per cent against). However, the devaluation of the pound on 18 September 1949 led to food price rises of 7 per cent by June 1950 while male wages rose by only 1 per cent. At the 1950 TUC the General Council's policy of continuing to support the White Paper led to its first defeat by Congress for many years, the critical motion passed (by 51.4 to 48.6 per cent of the votes cast) complained that prices and profits had risen while real wages had fallen.

The trade unions' collective response to the problem of sustaining and improving real wages was to try to promote industrial productivity. In 1948–9 the TUC promoted eight productivity conferences, involving unions in shipbuilding and engineering, cotton, pottery, chemicals, furniture and rubber. The TUC continued to press for more rapid productivity growth when the Conservatives returned to power (Booth, 1996). It was sharply critical of the Conservative government's pre-election tax cuts in 1955, the General Council complaining in its annual report that in being critical it 'had in mind the failure of Britain's exports to rise as much as those of Japan, Germany and other competitors and the continuing need to increase production and investment in industry'.

The Eden government (1955–7) addressed the problem of inflation with its White Paper, *The Economic Implications of Full Employment* (Cmd. 9725). After observing that no satisfactory solution had been found for the problem of 'continually rising prices', it stated:

If the prosperous economic conditions necessary to maintain full employment are exploited by trade unions and businessmen, price stability and full employment become incompatible. The solution lies in self-restraint in making wage claims and fixing profit margins and prices, so that total money income rises no faster than total output.

Earlier, in 1954, a Court of Inquiry into engineering and shipbuilding disputes had commented that individual wage demands were not a major problem but large claims which were part of 'a more general movement of wages, costs and prices... could conceivably undermine our whole economy'. It suggested that 'an authoritative and impartial body' should assess major wage claims 'to form a view upon their implication for the national economy and our ability to maintain our present standards'. Two further courts of inquiry into engineering and shipbuilding in 1957 repeated this suggestion.

In 1957 Peter Thorneycroft, Chancellor of the Exchequer, took up this suggestion, appointing the Council on Prices, Productivity and Incomes, otherwise known as the Cohen Committee or 'The Three Wise Men'. It consisted of Lord Cohen, a judge, Sir Harold Howitt, an accountant, and Sir Dennis Robertson, an economist. Neither Robertson nor Thorneycroft were committed to full employment, Robertson telling the Chancellor at the outset that he believed unemployment would need to rise in order to curb inflation. The Council's *First Report* (1958) condemned 'the habit of demanding large and frequent increases in monetary rewards' which persisted 'after any technical justification for it in the state of the labour market has passed away'. The trade unions were outraged by what they felt to be a one-sided condemnation of them and a readiness to accept higher unemployment. They also saw the Council on Prices, Productivity and Incomes as reinforcing Thorneycroft's more monetarist economic policies. Thorneycroft told the 1957 Conservative Party Conference: 'Honest money is a pre-requisite of full employment and good wages.' However, Thorneycroft and his Treasury colleagues resigned in January 1958 when Harold Macmillan and his Cabinet refused to hold down firmly the level of public expenditure in the year leading up to a general election.

The best remembered and most significant intervention over incomes by the Conservatives in office, 1951–64, came in 1961 with the 'pay pause' of Selwyn Lloyd, the Chancellor of the Exchequer. The Council on Prices, Productivity and Incomes in its *Fourth Report* (1961) had highlighted 'the extent to which earnings are actually being fixed locally, and the greater bargaining power on the floor of the shop that goes with this' and that rises in pay and profits should not outstrip increases in productivity. The Council recommended that projections should be made of future economic growth and this should be 'a guide for those responsible in their own particular fields for the planning of production, the fixing of prices and profit margins and the settlement of wages and salaries'. Selwyn Lloyd responded by telling the House of Commons that 'at present we are heavily overdrawing on our productivity account' and that in the public sector he required, with regard to pay, 'a pause until productivity has caught up'. He sugared this bitter pill by stating that during the pause he would consult both sides of industry. The wage pause was followed by a 'guiding light', which set 2–2.5 per cent rises as the maximum for April 1962 to March 1963, followed by 3–3.5 per cent for the subsequent two years. The TUC, while hostile to the public sector pay freeze, welcomed the Chancellor's intention 'to discuss with both sides of industry the implications of setting targets for planned increases of output'.

Seventeen years after the end of the Second World War, and after repeatedly requesting to be consulted, the trade union leadership became involved in discussing national economic planning. The forum for these discussions was the National Economic Development Council (NEDC), which met from March 1961. It consisted of trade unionists, employers and 'independent persons' and was chaired by the Chancellor. This was seen by the TUC as an alternative to 'a body with its own resources which could work and put forward a national plan'. By the summer of 1962 the Prime Minister, Harold Macmillan, believed that the 1961 measures had been inadequate and decided to introduce a formal incomes policy. After sacking Selwyn Lloyd and six other Cabinet ministers, Macmillan declared in July 1962: 'An incomes policy is... necessary as a permanent feature of our economic life', and set up the National Incomes Commission. The TUC, which had declined to discuss incomes policies on the National Economic Development Council, boycotted it. They opposed such a body intervening in specific wage settlements, thereby undermining free collective bargaining, and further argued it was one-sided for such action to target wages but not profits and prices.

With a Labour government in power, 1964–70, the trade unions were pleased to discuss the National Plan, provided such planning did not affect free collective bargaining. Harold Wilson's government secured TUC and employer support for its joint statement of intent on productivity, prices and incomes which included the aim of keeping prices stable. In setting up the National Board for

Prices and Incomes the government declared its intention 'to give the voluntary method every chance of proving that it can be made to work', but in so doing explicitly stated it relied on 'persuasion and the pressure of public opinion' to achieve stable prices and incomes. The voluntary approach collapsed with the July 1966 economic crisis. The failure to devalue the pound undercut the National Plan. A statutory prices and incomes policy was an important part of the government's emerging package of measures. The government introduced a six-month standstill for prices and incomes and, under the Prices and Incomes Act, 1966, set up the National Board for Prices and Incomes to report on proposed rises in prices and incomes referred to it by government ministers. Harold Wilson, addressing the TUC on 5 September 1966, warned: 'Restraint in incomes, an incomes policy related to productivity, is our only guarantee against unemployment.' He added: 'Over the past ten years every stop phase in the stop–go rhythm was marked by higher and higher unemployment figures.' The prices and incomes policy called for pay settlements to be annual or at longer intervals. From late 1967 a 3.5 per cent ceiling for wage, salary and dividend increases was set, with genuine productivity improvements being excepted. The policy was eased, with a range of 2.5 to 4.5 per cent set, but the policy lapsed in January 1970. In 1969 the government noted of the policy that such policies 'for short-term purposes can only have a short-term effect', adding that the 'long-term role of the policy is essentially an educational one'.

Edward Heath's Conservative government (1970–4) continued to consult the trade unions on the economy and, at first, did not introduce a statutory incomes policy. However, its Industrial Relations Act, 1971, undermined its relations with the trade union movement. It is sometimes suggested that the Heath government operated an incomes policy only from 1972. This is incorrect, as the Heath government, like previous post-war Conservative governments, applied curbs to the public sector, in this case making an attempt to ensure that each public sector pay award was 1 per cent less than the previous one for that group (a policy known as the '*N* minus one' policy).

In the second half of 1972 Heath was unable to secure TUC support for a voluntary incomes policy, so he went ahead with a statutory policy. This was more sophisticated than the previous policies in its coverage and its details. Its Stage Three, from November 1973, tried to remove wage bargainers' guesses as to future rises in inflation by providing threshold indexing (i.e. automatic wage increases each time prices passed certain levels), a policy which proved disastrous when oil and other goods escalated in price in the international economy. Stage One of Heath's incomes policy froze pay, prices, dividends and rents between November 1972 and April 1973. Stage Two, which ran until November 1973, allowed maximum pay rises of a £1 a week (a flat rate being to help the lower paid) plus 4 per cent up to a maximum of £250 per annum. Stage Three offered more flexibility than previous incomes policies, permitting pay increases of up to 7 per cent on the total pay for a group of employees (thereby allowing pay negotiators to determine the distribution), or for each person to receive up to £2.25 per week or 7 per cent up to a maximum of £350 per annum. In addition Stage Three allowed a margin of 1 per cent for productivity, sick-pay schemes or holiday entitlements. It also introduced the threshold agreements which were set at an increase in pay of £0.40 per week for every percentage point that the Retail Price Index rose above 7 per cent. In spite of the elaborate nature of this incomes policy, it broke down when the coal-miners insisted on a higher than 7 per cent pay award to restore what they had lost in relative pay since the settlement after the 1972 miners' strike. Edward Heath and his government refused to treat the miners as a special case and were not moved by TUC pledges that other unions would not use a concession to the miners as a precedent to argue rises for others. In the ensuing general election the Conservatives lost their majority in the House of Commons.

The final twentieth-century British attempt at operating an incomes policy came with the Labour governments of Harold Wilson, 1974–6, and James Callaghan, 1976–9. The main feature of this period was that incomes policies were part of a wider statutory and social package but with the economic details building on the complexities of Stage Three of Heath's policies. The trade unions were relieved to have the 1971 Industrial Relations Act repealed and replaced with legislation which drew on the more-positive-for-trade-unions aspects of the 1968 Donovan Report (see chapter 6). This legislation was part of a social package known as the Social Contract, which offered progress on 'the social wage' (welfare, pensions, housing) while money wages were controlled. Phase One of the Social Contract, which operated from July 1975 to July 1976, like Heath's policy, operated a flat rate pay increase to help the lower paid but this was set at £6 per week, with no increases for those earning over £8,500. Phase Two, running from July 1976 to July 1977, permitted pay rises of up to 5 per cent, but with a £2.50 per week minimum and a £4.00 per week maximum. Phases One and Two were agreed with the TUC. Thereafter, Phases Three and Four were unilaterally devised by James Callaghan's government. Phase Three set a maximum pay target of 10 per cent per annum, with self-financing productivity agreements, for 1977–8 but with Phase Four was overambitious in reducing the maximum pay target to 5 per cent for 1978–9. A further aspect of these incomes policies was Denis Healey, the Chancellor of the Exchequer, making part of proposed cuts in taxation (£900 of £1,200 million in the 1976 budget and £900 of £1,300 million in the 1977 budget) conditional on there being lower wage settlements.

The economic effects of incomes policies

Incomes policies were associated with Keynesian economics and the prioritising of full employment. The dangers of near full employment were seen to be a lack of constraint on trade union pressure on wages, which would lead to higher prices unless there was voluntary restraint or state intervention. The economist G. N. Worswick commented: 'Wage bargaining in full employment is, in fact, a political problem, and will be settled on the political plane' (Worswick, 1944).

The relationship between unemployment and wages was given theoretical underpinning by Professor A. W. Phillips in 1958. Drawing on statistics for 1861–1913 he suggested that there was an inverse relationship between the rate of change of money wages and the level of unemployment, which when depicted on a graph revealed a curve (Phillips, 1958). The Phillips Curve could be used to reinforce the control of pay by incomes policies but it also could be used to argue for non-Keynesian approaches, notably to operate demand-management policies which allowed unemployment to rise and curb inflation. Phillips' analysis was especially influential in the 1960s when the Phillips Curve provided a reasonably good fit for unemployment and wages during 1948–66. However, after this period, Britain and other industrialised countries experienced 'stagflation' (high unemployment, high prices and economic stagnation) and attempts to justify incomes policies with a modified, or augmented, Phillips Curve, were less influential.

By the late 1970s the argument that demand-management policies which curbed inflation (and trade union power) by allowing unemployment to rise was advocated by leading Conservatives and more economists. Margaret Thatcher's governments rejected formal incomes policies, relying instead on 'cash limits' in the public sector. As the economist Michael Artis has written: 'There is the point that the government is, directly and indirectly, a very large employer in the United Kingdom, that there must always be an incomes policy in that sense' (Artis, 1981, 19). Curbs on the public sector, with faith that the private sector would follow, were notable features of Conservative governments' policies in 1955–64 and 1970–2 as well as 1979 and after. Such policies often had adverse labour market effects. For example, in the 1980s and 1990s cash curbs combined with excessive auditing and form-filling, undercutting professional and public esteem, resulted in large-scale exits of teachers and problems in recruiting new staff.

The incomes policies of 1948–79 often lost support through a widespread view that they hit hardest the lowest paid groups with least 'industrial muscle'. In the public sector there was often national-level collective bargaining, with the government readily policing its own incomes policy, while in the private sector, where plant-level bargaining was more widespread, evasion was common. Indeed, in periods of shortage of skilled labour, employers were often very keen to hold on to their existing skilled labour and even to attract more at a time of good business. An early example of the government giving a lead to the private sector by squeezing groups unlikely to strike occurred in 1957 when the government reduced Whitley Council recommendations on pay increases for National Health Service and local government workers.

The widespread view that the earlier incomes policies were especially unfair on the lower paid resulted in the later attempts to remedy this with flat rate rises in 1972–4 and most successfully in 1975–9 (Steele, 1981). However, such treatment could disrupt pay differentials, with skilled labour becoming disgruntled at the erosion

opposed the Social Contract.
cial Contract, conceding that
ut added: 'I was against it be-
fect of reducing or lowering
probably was a minus for my

of the gap between unskilled and skilled wages. More generally support for incomes policies weakened as more people felt that they were unjust. Even with outright freezes on pay rises, anomalies occurred. Once policies moved away from the clarity of a freeze, groups of workers felt aggrieved at others doing better or, more generally, that their real wages were being reduced by rising prices. After a while support for the policies evaporated and groups of workers pressed successfully for big pay awards which 'caught up' at least part of the money lost during the effective part of the incomes policy period. As a result policy makers came to see the importance of ensuring that the incomes policy period was marked by higher real wages in order to avoid a wages explosion to catch up. As several economists had commented on the importance of take-home pay in employees' attitudes, one policy response, made by Denis Healey, was to offer conditional tax cuts (Artis, 1981, 115).

There has been much debate as to whether such catching up negates any early benefit arising from incomes policies. There were large pay claims, notably in the public sector, in 1969–70, 1974 and 1978–9, towards the end of incomes policies. Yet, even in these instances, there was the benefit that the incomes policies stopped wage bargaining becoming established as a more frequent event than once a year.

There is general agreement that the more successful incomes policies in reducing the rate of change of wages were those applied in times of economic crisis when the general public, including ordinary trade unionists, as well as trade union leaders supported the policies. This was so in 1948–50 and 1975–8. In 1948–50 real wages fell, with economic studies of the period suggesting that weekly wage rates were 2 per cent lower than they would have been otherwise. However, even so there were, as Russell Jones has commented, ominous developments: 'a notable growth in "wage drift", or payment by results, and company and plant bargaining' (Jones, 1987, 46). In 1975–77 the Social Contract played a major role in achieving a deceleration in wage increases for two successive years and securing an annual rate of increase to under 10 per cent. Although there are other causes of this success, such as stable international commodity prices, a rising exchange rate, monetary and fiscal policies, and a rise in unemployment, the Social Contract rightly took much credit for the fall in the rate of inflation from 24 to 8 per cent (while the

rise in weekly earnings was reduced from a rate of 27 t‹
per annum) (Davies, 1963, 441–3; Fishbein, 1984, 17

There is less agreement on the economic impact of
of 1961–74. Assessments of the Selwyn Lloyd and the
ernment policies have varied between suggesting that t
a 0 to a 1.15 per cent reduction in the rate of incre‹
wages. There was also an increase in productivity, pe
cent (Mitchell, 1972, 262). A stronger case for a subs
can be made if the incomes policies are divided int‹
'softer' phases. In the harder phases of 1961–2, 1966-
there were significant drops in the rate of increase of
However, in 1973 Heath's Stage Two of his incor
blown off course by his government's rapid increase
supply and also by soaring world commodity prices
435 and 442–4; Brown, 1976; Flanagan *et al.*, 198

There have also been disagreements on whether
a reduction in strike activity during incomes poli
found for the period 1966–75 that during the 'ha
comes policies there were reductions in strikes o
but an increase in stoppages over non-pay matter
However, there were upsurges of strikes at the
policies.

For the 1964–70 period, at least, incomes pol
ductivity bargaining. Many writers on the subj‹
such bargaining as simply a device whereby t
restraint could be evaded and extra money se
seeking genuine improvements. The one detai
on 62 of 3,000 cases) found that nearly hal
sulted in agreements with substantial productiv
McIntosh, 1973). Hence the comment in one ‹
pact of incomes policies on the private sector:
[National Board for Prices and Incomes] m
the impact of a superior management consult
1981, 96).

The policy appeal of incomes policies has b
ing 'fairness in adversity', requiring to have v
trade union) support for dealing with a ma
(as after 1945 and alarming levels of infl‹
1970s). Incomes policies have disintegrated

having restraints on pay rises. He als‹
In his autobiography he praised the S
it 'undoubtedly saved the economy',
cause the overall package had the e
differentials still further, so I think it
own union' (Jenkins, 1990, 141).

Chapter 6

Trade union legislation 1945–2000

For most of three and a half decades after the Second World War, British trade unionism had considerable freedom to act without fear of civil actions in the law courts under the Trade Disputes Act, 1906. This freedom was curtailed during the World Wars, under the Trade Disputes and Trade Union Act, 1927 (which was repealed by the Trade Union Act, 1946), by the Industrial Relations Act, 1971 (mostly repealed by the Trade Union and Labour Relations Act, 1974), and by a plethora of legislation in 1980–93. The legislation of the last three decades of the twentieth century came largely in response to concerns about trade union power affecting price stability, employment levels and economic growth, but concerns over freedom of individual choice were also expressed.

The flexibility of the voluntary nature of the British system of industrial relations was much admired by many academic commentators, most trade unionists and substantial numbers of employers after the Second World War. Otto Kahn-Freund, the eminent scholar of British, comparative and international labour law who had left Germany in 1933, contrasted very favourably the 'dynamic' British system with the 'static' systems elsewhere, notably in Weimar Germany (1918–33), other parts of Europe and the United States, which were tied up in legal contracts and regulations. (Kahn-Freund, 1954). As a member of the 1965–8 Royal Commission on Trade Unions and Employers' Associations (the Donovan Commission), he and other members found that circumstances had altered and that there was a need to respond to the results of the decentralisation of pay bargaining, which had been brought about by changed business strategies, and also to the growth in power of shop stewards. Furthermore, there was the problem of a substantial increase in the number of unofficial strikes (Clegg, 1983).

The Donovan Report declared that there were two systems of industrial relations in Britain. There was 'the formal system embodied in the official institutions' and there was 'the informal system created by the actual behaviour of trade unions and employers' associations, of managers, shop stewards and workers'. The Donovan Report noted that the 'decentralisation of collective bargaining has taken place under the pressure of full employment, which in Britain has had special consequences because of the way our industrial organisations have reacted to it' (Royal Commission, 1968, 261).

The majority Report called for reforms to the British system of industrial relations but preferred that these should reinforce the voluntary system, with only a limited role for the law. In this view, what was needed was to persuade people to change their procedures for dealing with industrial disputes. Factory-wide agreements were called for, while industry-wide agreements should only be for 'those matters which they can effectively regulate'. The majority report did call for legislation to require large companies to register their collective agreements and to set up an Industrial Relations Commission whose tasks would include 'carrying out inquiries into the general state of industrial relations in a factory or industry'. It was further stated: 'These proposals will assist an incomes policy to work effectively by exposing the whole process of pay settlement to the influence of policy' (Royal Commission, 1968, 262–4).

Harold Wilson's Labour government (1964–70) adopted much of the Donovan Report but chose to go further in a few respects. It set up a Commission on Industrial Relations to promote the spread of collective bargaining and good industrial relations, still within a voluntary system (a requirement of the TUC for support). The government brought forward a White Paper, *In Place of Strife: A Policy For Industrial Relations* (Cmnd. 3888), in January 1969 which proposed twenty-five proposals, mostly following the Donovan Report's recommendations. Most were welcomed by the trade unions. However, three proposals led to considerable controversy between the Labour government and the trade unions and also within the Labour Party, which had been considered and rejected by the Donovan Commission. These measures, requiring statutory enforcement, were to give the Secretary of State the power to order compulsory ballots before major strikes and to order a 'cooling-off period' in unofficial strikes or where it was deemed inadequate joint discussions had occurred; and, in addition, there were to be legally binding references to the Commission on Industrial Relations to resolve inter-union disputes. Eric Heffer, a prominent Left-wing MP, complained of the first two measures and of the fines which could be attached from trade unionists' wages. He wrote at the time:

These proposals add up to a new type of interference by government in industrial relations . . . In a sense, it is an extension of the state intervention begun in the Prices and Incomes Act, and is in line with the new concept of state control.

(Quoted in Wrigley, 1997, 82)

The *In Place of Strife* proposals were criticised as inadequate by the Confederation of British Industry (CBI) and the Conservative Party.

The Labour government failed to legislate as it had proposed in *In Place of Strife* and was defeated in the 1970 general election. Edward Heath's Conservative government (1970–4) did legislate in 1971. Its Industrial Relations Act drew not on the Donovan Report but on Conservative policies which had been evolving during the previous two decades. After a very emollient approach to the trade unions under Churchill in opposition (1945–51) and in office (1951–5), a more critical approach was outlined by the Inns of Court Conservative and Unionist Society (set up in 1947) in its influential pamphlet, *A Giant's Strength* (1958). This policy document argued for legal restrictions on trade union power, in particular measures against the closed shop, restrictive practices, secondary strikes and demarcation disputes.

The intentions of the Trade Disputes Act, 1906, were undermined by the House of Lords judgement in 1964 on the *Rookes v. Barnard* case. Douglas Rookes, an employee of British Overseas Airways Corporation's design offices at London airport, resigned from his union, the Draughtsmen's and Allied Technicians' Association (DATA), in 1955 in disgust at his union's failure to take more vigorous action in a dispute over working conditions. He had been a trade union activist, even being involved in securing a closed shop agreement in 1954. After he lost his job following his union's threat to strike to enforce the closed shop, he sued the union for damages, winning £7,500 (Rookes, 1966). This was followed in 1965 by the case of *Stratford v. Lindley*, which also undercut immunities hitherto believed to be given by the Trade Disputes Act, 1906, in this instance relating to secondary boycotting (Davies and Freedland, 1993, 243–6).

The Inns of Court Conservative and Unionist Society built on the *Rookes v. Barnard* judgement to state in their evidence in February 1966 to the Donovan Commission that the trade unions should be brought within the law. They also set out a lengthy list of proposals, mostly taken up later in the Industrial Relations Act 1971. These proposals, published as *Trade Unions For Tomorrow* (1966) in pamphlet form, included registration of trade union constitutions and rules, the creation of a National Industrial Relations Court, banning of sympathetic strikes, closed shops only by agreement with employers and then safeguarding of a right for individuals not to be trade union members, and breach of collective agreements to be subject to legal redress. This was reformulated in the Conservative Political Centre's *Fair Deal At Work* (1968). These proposals drawn up in Opposition provided the basis for the Industrial Relations Act, 1971.

The Industrial Relations Act, 1971, marked a major change in the law and industrial relations. It was a turning away from the post-Second World War basic principle of English labour law described by Otto Kahn-Freund as 'collective laissez-faire'. It repealed the whole of the Trade Union Act, 1871, the Trade Union Amendment Act, 1876, the Trade Disputes Act, 1906 and the Trade Disputes Act, 1965 (which had reversed the House of Lords' judgement on *Rookes v. Barnard*) as well as parts or all of fourteen other Acts. Unlike Margaret Thatcher's government which legislated in stages, the Heath government brought in one huge measure, which had eight parts, 170 sections and nine schedules. Stemming from the Conservative lawyers, who had been influenced by US labour law, its main drafter was Sir Geoffrey Howe, the Solicitor-General, who claimed that 'the major part of the Government's proposals are directly in line with Donovan's recommendations' (McCarthy, 1992, 18–21).

However, if its aims were similar to those of the Donovan Report, its construction of a comprehensive legal framework for industrial relations, with penalties for a range of actions, was an approach rejected by the majority on the Commission. Among ideas considered and rejected by the Donovan Commission was compulsory cooling-off periods. These were introduced under the 1971 Act. This power was only used once, in April 1972, over a threatened rail strike for increased pay. Maurice Macmillan, the Secretary of State for Employment, secured a fourteen-day cooling-off period and a secret ballot from the National Industrial Relations Court. However, over 80 per cent of the railway workers who voted backed the union in demanding a greater than 11 per cent rise, with the result that the employers conceded 13 per cent. This episode confirmed the Donovan view that such ballots were likely to do no more than strengthen the union leaders' bargaining position. The operation of the law against dockers carrying out secondary action also backfired. Five shop stewards were sent to Pentonville prison for continuing to picket another container depot after the National Industrial Relations Court had ordered such action should stop. A one-day general strike was avoided by the House of Lords making the union liable for the action of its stewards, resulting in a fine for the union but the release of the 'Pentonville Five'.

Edward Heath and his ministerial colleagues attached great importance to securing the registration of most trade unions under the 1971 Act. They saw to it that the Act offered many advantages, such as much immunity from legal action over strikes, to those that did register. However, the TUC's strategy of boycotting registration under the Act substantially undermined the Act. Equally damaging was the unwillingness of most employers to make use of the Act. Heath was dismayed during the February 1974 general election campaign when Campbell Adamson, the Director General of the Confederation of British Industry (CBI), expressed the view that the Industrial Relations Act had embittered industrial relations and should be scrapped.

Academic assessments have also been unfavourable. A major study by Weekes, Mellish, Dickens and Lloyd (1975) found that bargaining reform had not been affected by the 1971 Act. Private and public sector employers alike readily inserted a clause into agreements: 'This is not a legally enforceable agreement' (known among some trade unionists as a TINA LEA). They also found that only a few non-TUC unions sought recognition, these representing only some 5,000 members, and there were little changes to union rule books, even by those few unions which did register. Overall the 1971 Act was a failure in reducing strikes. McCarthy points to a fall in the number in 1971, which he suggests may have been due to a rise in unemployment, but thereafter the number of strikes rose. However, the number of working days lost through strikes unequivocally shot up, 1972's number only being exceeded by 1926 (the year of the General Strike and lengthy coal dispute) and was accompanied by massive rises in pay (McCarthy, 1992, 22–4).

With the return to office of the Labour Party in 1974, there was soon legislation restoring the voluntaristic approach to industrial relations. The Trade Union and Labour Relations Acts, 1974 and 1976, repealed the Industrial Relations Act, 1971, except for the part dealing with unfair dismissals, and enacted new versions of the 1871–1965 legislation which had been deleted from the statute book in 1971. The Employment Protection Act, 1975, drew on the principles of the Donovan Report. It included six provisions to foster trade union recognition and the spread of collective bargaining. It restored the closed shop, but with a conscience clause enabling exceptions. It also provided a range of rights, such as maternity leave and remedies for unfair dismissal.

The Employment Protection Act, 1975, gave statutory powers to the Advisory, Conciliation and Arbitration Service (ACAS), a tripartite body which arose from talks between the TUC and CBI in 1972 and which operated from 1974. ACAS offered conciliation and advice, published codes of practice and (until the Employment Act, 1980) could try to ensure trade union recognition by employers. ACAS strengthened the voluntary system, and it was itself free from ministerial interference. The Employment Act, 1975, also set up the Central Arbitration Committee and a certification officer (in place of the registrar under the 1971 Act) (Kessler and Bayliss, 1998, 29–31).

The impact of the 1974–6 legislation was mixed. ACAS was a success, though it appears to have not greatly increased trade union recognition. Many low-paid workers benefited from references to the Central Arbitration Committee; they were most of the 150,000 workers who gained increases of pay that way by 1978. However, in spite of the intentions of the Employment Act, 1975, those found to have been unfairly dismissed received low levels of compensation and were very rarely reinstated. The removal of the legal restraints of 1971–4 did not lead to an explosion in the number of strikes, indeed the number of strikes, strikers and days lost fell well below the 1974 level. That is until early 1979, the so-called 'winter of discontent' (McCarthy, 1992, 30–9). The Conservative Party was highly critical of the Employment Protection Bill. Jim Prior commented in the House of Commons:

> The Bill contains no obligation on unions to avoid strikes, to keep to contracts, to respect the public interest, to promote greater efficiency through increased productivity, to provide more flexible training methods or to provide greater mobility of labour . . .
>
> A more appropriate name for the Bill would be the Trade Union Benefits (No. 2) Bill.

Employers' organisations complained to the Department of Employment. The *Times* reporting the meeting commented: 'The clear suggestion from the employers was that what was happening to them under the Bill's present provisions looked like the reverse of what happened to the trade unions under the Industrial Relations Act now repealed.' There were also growing doubts about the adequacy of voluntaryism among some of its earlier proponents. For instance, Otto Kahn-Freund observed: 'I am coming increasingly to the conclusion, outrageous from the Marxist point of view, that what the state represents is the consumer: in intention, not in actuality' (Wedderburn *et al.*, 1983, 121).

With the return to office of the Conservatives, the legal pendulum swung again, and there were eight major legislative measures dealing with trade unions and employment law, 1980–93. These were: the Employment Acts of 1980, 1982, 1988, 1989 and 1990; the Trade Union Act, 1984; the Wages Act 1986; and the Trade Union Reform and Employment Rights Act, 1993 (with a related ninth in the Sex Discrimination Act, 1986). With the 1980–93 legislation the Thatcher and Major governments changed laws relating to trade unions in stages rather than in one big measure as the Heath government had done in 1971. (The main provisions of these Acts are printed in Wrigley, 1997, 163–80.) Partly as a result of this approach, but probably because of the weakened economic circumstances of the trade unions and their lower public esteem after the strikes of 1979, there was less effective opposition.

Margaret Thatcher's and John Major's governments (1979–97), unlike the Conservative governments of 1951–64 and 1970–4, had no inclination towards frequent consultations with the trade unions, let alone to offering any corporatist involvement in running the economy. The National Economic Development Council was marginalised, its monthly meetings being reduced to quarterly ones in 1984, and it was axed with effect from 1 January 1993. Generally the trade unions were kept at a distance, with Margaret Thatcher's comment on the miners as 'the enemy within' being appropriate for her view of trade unionism generally. She, Norman Tebbitt and other Conservatives on the Right saw trade unions as serious impediments to a free market economy, adding to the cost of goods and services, and contributing to uncompetitiveness and to unemployment. Other distortions of the free market, in their eyes, were the 'safety net' provisions given to young and low-paid workers. In 1988 young workers (ages 16–21) were removed from the protection of wages councils, and in 1993 the councils themselves were abolished.

One major area affected by the trade union legislation was the ability of trade unions to engage in industrial disputes. Before strikes were called, the support of union members had to be secured by secret ballot (under the 1984 and 1988 Acts). The 1993 legislation went further, requiring that employers not only should be given seven days' notice of action, but that they be provided with lists of which employees would be involved and the date on which it would begin. Under the 1982 Act strikes were only legally protected if they concerned 'wholly or mainly' employment issues affecting those involved and their own employer. Also, under the 1980 legislation, picketing was only lawful at the strikers' own workplace. The 1982 and 1988 Acts made pressure to enforce closed shops illegal.

A second major area of the legislation regulated trade union government and gave members' rights against their own unions. The 1984 and 1988 legislation required regular, secret ballots for all principal officer posts and also executive committee members of unions. The 1980 Act gave those seeking work the right not to be refused membership on unreasonable grounds and to be eligible for financial compensation through an industrial tribunal should this happen. The 1988 legislation gave union members the right to demand a ballot before industrial action and not to be disciplined if they refused to take part in any such action. It also established a Commissioner for the Rights of Trade Union Members to provide advice and financial assistance to any member who wished to take legal action against their own union. The 1988 legislation also banned union funds being used to indemnify trade union officials who carried out union instructions which proved unlawful.

A third major area of the legislation removed or restricted previous employee rights against employers. There was a repeal of all rights for those unfairly dismissed within two years of starting employment somewhere, including no requirement to provide reasons for dismissal (under the 1989 legislation), and repeal of some rights of those dismissed because of taking unofficial strike action (under the 1990 legislation). There was narrowing of maternity rights (by the 1980 Act) and of time off for trade union duties (by the 1989 Act). There was also removal of protective regulations from various groups of labour: an ending of preventing women working underground or taking on 'heavy work' or being restricted in working nights; de-restricting young persons' hours of work (under the 1989 legislation) and removing them from the scope of wages councils (by the 1986 Act); de-restricting the baking industry's hours of work (by repealing a 1954 Act); and banning public authorities insisting on minimum employment terms as a condition of granting contracts (Local Government Act, 1988).

A fourth major area of the legislation ended various aids to union recognition and to extending collective bargaining. The 1980 Employment Act repealed the right to refer a claim for trade union recognition to ACAS, with the possibility of an award by the Central Arbitration Committee, and also abolished the procedure whereby trade unions could secure a binding award from Central Arbitration Committee when they could show employers were not observing recognised terms and conditions. The 1982 Employment Act made it illegal to make it a requirement in contracts that work be carried out by trade unionists or that contractors must recognise or negotiate with trade unionists. The 1993 legislation protected employers from legal action if they gave trade union members lower wages than non-trade unionists. It also took away from ACAS the duty of encouraging the extension of collective bargaining (McCarthy, 1992, 42–8; Wrigley, 1997, 163–80).

As with other trade union and industrial relations legislation, it is not always clear which subsequent changes are due to the legislation and which to other changed circumstances. The legislation of 1980–93 came at a time when international and national economic circumstances were not favourable to trade unionism. There were similar declines in trade union membership and in levels of strike activity in other industrialised countries, several of which had not introduced similar legislation. In Britain the lessening of strike activity and some aspects of the weakening of trade union membership were apparent before the legislation took effect.

However, when explaining periods of rapid expansion of trade unionism, the case is often made that success breeds success and that political circumstances favourable to trade unionism are important as well as economic circumstances. In 1979–97 political circumstances were very unfavourable for much of the period, with Margaret Thatcher and several of her colleagues not concealing their detestation of trade unionism and of most trade union leaders. Adverse economic and political circumstances substantially lowered expectations of benefits from union membership. Indeed, membership seemed to offer a greater likelihood of individuals being on a fast track to redundancy, leading to further weakening of support. To change the political climate for trade unionism and to reduce expectations of the benefits from trade union membership were intentions of the framers of the 1980–93 legislation and, to a large extent, these aims were fulfilled.

The 1980–93 legislation was a second attempt to move from voluntaryism to a framework of law for industrial relations. The first attempt, with the 1971 Industrial Relations Act, failed. There was a general belief that it led to industrial relations being more, not less, tumultuous. Trade unions successfully boycotted it and employers rarely took up its provisions, and then seldom against their own employees. In contrast, as John McInnes, a notable critic of the Thatcher government's policies, noted of the 1980s legislation:

In its early years of operation it successfully avoided creating 'martyrs' while effectively facing unions with crippling penalties if they lent official support to action which was unlawful. In part it was because the alternative of 'keeping the law out of industrial relations' was no longer credible.

(McInnes, 1987, 143)

In the 1980s employers in both the public and the private sector were prepared to use the law, especially in taking out injunctions. Over three years, 1984–7, employers sought 77 injunctions (with 73 granted), 65 against their own workforce. Of these, 47 related to pre-strike ballots, 16 to secondary action and 11 to picketing (Evans, 1987). Another study recorded 169 applications for injunctions between 1983 and 1996. A breakdown of part of the number revealed 62 related to pre-strike ballots, 36 to picketing and 32 to secondary action, with the number for picketing and secondary action being notably high in the 1980s (Gall and MacKay, 1996; Kessler and Bayliss, 1998, 85–6).

The unions receiving the greatest number of injunctions were the print unions, whose closed shops were demolished in the mid 1980s, notably in confrontations with Eddie Shah's Messenger Group in the Manchester area and with Rupert Murdoch and News International in its move of its operations to Wapping. In these disputes injunctions were especially important, with fines and legal costs running over a million pounds. They added to unfavourable conditions for the print unions, faced with technological change, excess capacity in the industry and determined employers.

In the 1984–5 miners dispute the National Coal Board secured an injunction against secondary picketing in the Nottinghamshire area, but it was not enforced. In South Wales injunctions were taken out and enforced by a road haulage firm and by working miners. However, mass picketing was countered by arrests under criminal law or by police acting against what they believed to be future breaches of the peace (Kessler and Bayliss, 1998, 87–93). While the use of injunctions played a small part, the main contrast with 1972–4 was that the government was willing to see the whole coal industry go over the edge, and, as was shown subsequently, even to give it a push.

Overall, the 1980–93 legislation had an impact on strikes. Strike ballots became common and the trade unions adapted to often making effective use of them (see chapter 4). There was a decline in picketing generally, but very much so in secondary picketing. After a rash of injunctions in the mid 1980s, it appears to have become less of a problem for employers. The legislation made it very difficult for strong unions to help the weak, and so it has often been weaker unionised areas which have been most affected (McCarthy, 1992, 67–71).

The 1980–93 legislation was also intended to boost British industry's productivity. There had been hopes in the 1950s that productivity bargaining would deliver results under the voluntaryist system of industrial relations, with the example of agreements made at the Esso refinery at Fawley being heralded as the way forward. At Fawley two productivity agreements made in 1959 and 1963 had abolished overtime, raised output and increased the return on capital while giving the workforce a shorter working week and substantial increases in pay. However, this approach did not become a norm in British industry and a subsequent study of the Fawley oil refinery suggested that the productivity outcome in the longer term was not all that the legend suggested (Flanders, 1964; Ahlstrand, 1991). In the early 1980s there appears to have been an improved productivity in British manufacturing. In Britain the annual percentage changes to output per head in British manufacturing ran behind the average of seven major industrial countries in 1964–79 (3.8 to 5.0 in 1964–73 and 0.7 to 3.2 in 1973–9) but was better in 1980–86 (3.6 to 2.8)(Metcalf, 1989). Broadberry's major analysis of comparative productivity displays no decisive turn-around after 1980, the British decline lessening (Broadberry, 1997). Such improvements in output per head after 1979 may be explained in large part by the wholesale closures of much of British manufacturing industry, the closures removing much less efficient plant and firms. The period 1980–93 was not notable for resolving long-standing skills shortages in British industry.

The 1980–93 legislation removed protection from many groups of workers, thereby aiming to provide a more flexible labour force. Such studies as have been made of this have shown the conditions of the workers concerned have deteriorated but have not found evidence of substantial benefits for employers (McCarthy, 1992, 59–60).

Overall, the 1980–93 legislation was 'step by step' or even ad hoc in its approach. Margaret Thatcher and some of her colleagues were much impressed by the ideas of Hayek, and his ideas have been much discussed in relation to her government's policies (for example, Tomlinson, 1990). Lord Wedderburn and others have portrayed the legislation of 1980–93 as a decisive break with the past, owing much of its overall conception to Hayek (McCarthy, 1992). Simon Auerbach in a major study of the Thatcher government's legislation has argued that it represented more a 'patchwork' of influences and that these stem from the politics of the time rather than an ideological blueprint (Auerbach, 1990). This sense of politics determining statutory outcomes influenced Tony Blair's decision to maintain much of the legislation. After taking office he commented: 'there will be no going back. The days of strikes without ballots, mass picketing, closed shops and secondary action are over'.

However, in 1998, a year after the Labour Party's election victory, the Blair government published a White Paper, *Fairness At Work*. This set out a statutory framework for trade union recognition, a legal right for trade union representation in individual disciplinary or grievance cases, simplification of the law on strike ballots and better maternity rights among its proposals. Tony Blair commented of the proposals that even with them becoming law the UK would remain 'the most lightly regulated labour market of any leading economy'.

The Employment Relations Act, 1999, gave legislative effect to *Fairness At Work*, with its centre piece on union recognition coming into effect in June 2000 (nearly twenty years after the previous legal right to recognition was abolished). Under this Act unions can formally request recognition. If there is no voluntary agreement then the trade union can go to the Central Arbitration Committee, which can encourage further negotiations. If these fail, then there can be an award of recognition if more than half the workforce is in the union and they wish for recognition. Alternatively, the Central Arbitration Committee can arrange the holding of a ballot, which will result in union recognition if 40 per cent of those entitled to vote do so and if over 50 per cent of those voting vote in favour. Where unions fail to secure recognition after approaching the Central Arbitration Committee, they are barred from seeking recognition for this bargaining unit or a substantially similar group of employees for three years.

After the first year the Central Arbitration Committee's annual report (July 2001) observed that the trade unions 'seem generally to have avoided bringing cases in which they were not highly confident of both their level of membership and the degree of support for recognition in the proposed bargaining unit'. Over half of the first applications were for groups of under 100 employees, the unions deeming it difficult to secure recognition for large groups of workers employed over several sites. However, the existence of the legislation encouraged more employers to make voluntary agreements.

The Employment Relations Act, 1999, also included the extension of maternity rights from 14 to 18 weeks, new rights for part-time workers, some protection from employer blacklists and the right to unpaid time-off for urgent domestic incidents. Some of these areas of legislation followed European directives. By the end of the twentieth century the pace of change was often being encouraged, if not made, by the European Union. In 2001, for instance, the European information and consultation directive required that within three years undertakings with at least fifty employees regularly consult their workforce on recent and probable future developments in their activities, their economic situation, likely changes in work organisation and possible redundancies.

The other major measure of the first term of the Blair government was the National Minimum Wage Act, 1998, which came into operation in April 1999. It set two minimum rates, which initially were £3.60 an hour for workers aged 22 or more and £3.00 an hour for workers aged 18 to 21. The legislation excluded those under 18, apprentices under 19 and older apprentices in the first year of apprenticeship, trainees on government schemes, people living and working with families (nannies and au pairs), trainee teachers, members of the armed forces and the genuinely self-employed. While the unions warmly welcomed the introduction of a minimum wage, there was disappointment it was set below £5 an hour. On 10 April 1999 some 20,000 trade unions demonstrated in Newcastle for 'a Living Wage'. In February 2000, the Conservative Party which had vigorously opposed a minimum wage, announced it would not repeal it should it regain office. The government raised the main rate to £3.70 an hour in October 2000 and to £4.10 in October 2001, with the youth rate raised to £3.20 in June 2000. The legislation was enforced by the Inland Revenue and the Department of Trade and Industry. Between April 2000 and March 2001 nearly £3 million in wage arrears was secured for underpaid workers by wage compliance officers.

Chapter 7

What have trade unions done?

The role of trade unions in Western industrialised societies became a highly controversial issue in the last two decades of the twentieth century. In an age of widespread renewed belief in the efficacy of free market economies, many economists and politicians saw them as blocks on the working of the free market. In contrast, many people who desired protection in 'the flexible labour market' saw more their 'sword of justice' role. In 1984, after examining trade union activities in the USA, Freeman and Medoff, two Harvard economists, observed that unions had two faces, 'a monopoly face' and 'a voice/response face', and concluded:

If one looks only at the monopoly face, most of what trade unions do is socially harmful. If one looks at only the voice/response face, most of what unions do is socially beneficial.

(Freeman and Medoff, 1984, 246)

Freeman and Medoff in their study, *What Do Trade Unions Do?* focused on three areas of controversy: efficiency, distribution of income and social organisation. In their study of US trade unions they argued that trade unionism could lower employment levels but that 'in many settings it is associated with increased productivity'. On the issue of distribution of income they found that unions reduced inequality in wages and lowered profits. As for social organisation they did not substantiate the belief that unions were corrupt or undemocratic and found that politically 'unions, for the most part, provide political voice to all labor and that they are more effective in pushing general social legislation than in bringing about special interest legislation in the Congress'. They argued that personally, while favouring 'a thriving market economy', they also favoured a strong trade union movement and were 'concerned with the on-going decline in private sector unionism' (Freeman and Medoff, 1984, 247–8).

A later US study, edited by Mishel and Voos, argued that trade unions and collective bargaining were not responsible for the decline of American competitiveness. Mishel and Voos argued that where the USA had substantial trade deficits, such as with West Germany and Canada, those countries had higher wages. Where the USA was suffering from competition with countries with lower wages, such as Korea, Taiwan and Mexico, the wage levels in these countries were so low that the pay gap had 'very little to do with union wage premiums in the US'. They further argued,

Unionization is neither a necessary nor sufficient condition for the competitive disadvantages we observe. If unionization alone was sufficient, competitors with more heavily unionized workforces would also be suffering competitive disadvantages. However, unionization rates are far higher in other industrialized countries which are thriving in the international market . . .

If unionization were a necessary condition for our declining competitiveness, then nonunion industries should be unaffected. The declining competitive position of nonunion high-tech industries in the late 1980s makes it clear that there is no necessary connection.

(Mishel and Voos, 1992, 2–6)

Other studies in the same book provided statistical evidence on 360 industries which suggested unionisation was not a cause of the USA's deterioration in its balance of trade, and also evidence to indicate that 'there is no union effect – positive or negative – on technological modernization' (Karier and O'Keefe in Mishel and Voos, 1992, 15–39 and 109–41). With the levels of unionisation in the USA falling sooner and further than in the UK, it is interesting to see some such arguments emerging as it increasingly became less credible to ascribe various economic problems to union power in the labour market; or at least, as some have suggested, since the late 1960s.

In the UK trade unions had been longer established and had achieved a higher density of membership than in the USA. In the post-Second World War period the unions operated in a favourable labour market and, in the view of such an expert in labour economics as Henry Phelps Brown, played a baleful cost–push role in inflation (Phelps Brown, 1983, 147–67). N. F. R. Crafts in his influential study of post-1945 UK economic growth ascribed the major reason for relatively slow growth rates to poor productivity growth and highlighted supply side problems causing 'a relatively slow reduction of overmanning' and a slow achievement of 'the benefits from new technical possibilities in production'. In particular he blamed 'weak management, poor industrial relations, ineffective research and development, and low levels of vocational training'. Crafts also argued that the Thatcher government years had seen marked reductions in 'industrial relations obstacles to productivity enhancement' (Crafts, 1991, 287–9).

David Metcalf, who has written substantial work on the economic effects of trade unionism in Britain, wrote of the 1980s that workplaces with unions were associated with lower productivity and higher relative pay, so profitability was often lower in such establishments. He argued that rising labour productivity in manufacturing in the 1980s 'rests on fear, competition and decentralisation of collective bargaining'. However, he emphasised that 'the impact of unions is not independent of managerial behaviour' and commented: 'Unions are not homogenous and, for example, those organising skilled workers may have different effects than general unions'. Hence he urged that 'statistical analysis must be complemented by case-studies at workplace level'. He also took up Alan Flanders' suggestion that unions had 'a sword of justice' as well as a 'vested interest' effect (Metcalf, 1989, 21–22).

Metcalf has not been alone in emphasising more the 'sword of justice' side of trade unions in Britain for the late years of the twentieth century. With trade unions allegedly 'tamed' in the Thatcher–Major years, their density low in the private sector and relatively low levels of strike activity, it increasingly became unconvincing to lay major aspects of poor economic performance at their feet. However, in the 'golden age' of the international economy (roughly 1950–73) Britain's sluggish performance was marked by poor productivity and inefficient use of labour, and both management and labour were responsible for this.

In a recent survey Aldcroft and Oliver followed both Freeman and Medoff and Metcalf in seeing positive as well as negative economic effects of trade unions. On the negative side they observed:

If their activities became too disruptive or their bargaining stance too intransigent, then they could adversely affect investment, innovation, productivity growth and the cost-structure of industry, thereby weakening the country's competitive strength.

On the positive side, they commented:

They may galvanise lethargic management into action, they can monitor work processes and speak with a collective voice, while even shop stewards have been known to discipline recalcitrant workers. Strong wage pressure in highly unionised plants may also encourage employers to increase capital intensity and introduce more efficient work methods, both of which will raise productivity. Moreover, the union movement has by no means been implacably opposed to innovation and new techniques and the TUC has generally welcomed such change provided it can be managed in a socially acceptable way.

(Aldcroft and Oliver, 2000, 92)

In looking at the 'voice/response' face of trade unionism Freeman and Medoff emphasised their role in the distribution of income. They observed that for those 'to whom greater economic equality is a plus, what unions do here is definitely good' but for those 'to whom greater equalization of incomes is undesirable, what unions do is definitely bad' (Freeman and Medoff, 1984, 248). In Britain, as in the USA, the unions secured higher wages for union labour ('the union mark-up') than for non-union labour and were often successful in delaying, or even resisting, wage cuts. Estimates of the scale of the 'mark-up' in Britain have varied from a little above zero to as much as 70 per cent, with estimates based on aggregate data being generally higher than those based on data of more detailed studies. The British data from the Workplace Industrial Relations Surveys of the 1980s suggest considerable variety of union–non-union wage gaps. In the case of semi-skilled manual workers where product markets were competitive, there was no wage gap. In contrast, where there was multi-unionism combined with separate bargaining or where there were closed shops, there were higher than average wage gaps. However, there were also substantial wage gaps not due to unions, with many successful firms holding or attracting labour by paying more than their competitors (Booth, 1995, 169–70).

Union presence in British workplaces has been a force for equality. There has been less earnings dispersion, with unions pressing for equalisation of pay and conditions for members doing similar work. Union pressure achieved markedly better pay, a higher 'union mark-up', for lower-paid workers; for unskilled, female black and disabled workers. Estimates for 1982 suggested a narrowing of the wage gap between male skilled and unskilled of 2 per cent, between male manual and non-manual of 9 per cent, between female and male of 1 per cent and between black and white workers of 5 per cent (Metcalf, 1989, 32–4). A study at the end of the century suggested that unions narrowed the wage gap between female and male workers by 3 per cent (Metcalf *et al.*, 2000).

Trade unions have also had a less quantifiable but important impact in such matters as health and safety and the discouragement of the arbitrary treatment of employees by management. Such research that has been carried out on the relationship between trade union presence and accidents at work has shown a substantially lower number of accidents at unionised workplaces. The trade unions, as mentioned earlier (chapter 3), played a substantial role at the end of the century in representing their members at tribunals, and securing substantial sums of compensation for dismissals.

The trade unions have also displayed much altruism in campaigning on a variety of social and environmental issues. The 'Social Contract' of the mid 1970s included many social benefits, from housing issues to pensions. In the case of pensions the TUC has been at the forefront in supporting improved benefits. In its submission of a proposed budget in 2000 the TUC prioritised pensions (with two other matters), calling for £2 billion spending to end pensioner poverty. The 1999 TUC called upon the General Council to support the National Pensioners' Convention. The trade union movement also supplied two outstanding leaders to pensioner pressure groups, in Jack Jones and Rodney Bickerstaffe.

By the end of the twentieth century the British trade union movement was trying to reverse the substantial decline of membership over nearly two decades and to adjust to substantial changes in the labour market. The old manual/non-manual divisions in the workplace remained but were less substantial than between those in relatively secure full-time employment and the third of the labour force who were temporary, part-time or self-employed (Russell,

1998). The TUC still looked to the British government for changes favourable to employees. Increasingly, it also looked to Europe. John Monks, the TUC general secretary, noted in his report to the 2000 TUC that in many important areas 'the impetus for change comes from Europe, where we continue to play a leading role...in promoting and advancing the European social model as the way ahead, combining business success with high social standards'.

References

Ackers, P. (1995). 'Change in Trade Unions since 1945: a Response to Heery and Kelly'. *Work, Employment and Society*, 9.1.

Ackers, K. P., Smith, C. and Smith, P. (1996). *The New Workplace and Trade Unionism*. London, Routledge.

Ahlstrand, B. (1991). *The Quest for Productivity: A Study of Fawley after Flanders*. Cambridge University Press.

Aldcroft, D. H. and Oliver, M. J. (2000). *Trade Unions and the Economy, 1870–2000*. Aldershot, Ashgate. A substantial reassessment, often shrewd sometimes unconvincing.

Artis, M. (1981). 'Incomes Policies: some Rationales' in Fallick and Elliott (eds.).

Ashworth, W. (1985). *The History of the British Coal Industry*, vol. 5. Oxford, Clarendon Press.

Auerbach, Simon (1990). *Legislating for Conflict*. Oxford University Press. The best study of the Thatcher government's trade union legislation.

Bain, G. S. (1970). *The Growth of White-Collar Unionism*. Oxford, Clarendon Press. The classic analysis.

Bain, G. S. and Elsheikh, F. (1976). *Union Growth and the Business Cycle*. Oxford, Blackwell.

Bain, G. S. and Price, R. (1980). *Profiles of Union Growth*. Oxford, Blackwell. Very important trade union statistics, providing estimates of trade union densities.

Balfour, C. (1972). *Incomes Policy and the Public Sector*. London, Routledge and Kegan Paul.

Barnes, D. and Reid, E. (1980). *Governments And Trade Unions: The British Experience, 1964–79*. London, Heinemann Educational.

Bassett, Philip (1986). *Strike Free: New Industrial Relations in Britain*. London, Macmillan.

Beaumont, P. B. and Harris, R. I. D. (1988). 'Sub-systems of Industrial Relations: the Spatial Dimension in Britain'. *British Journal of Industrial Relations*, 26.

Blackaby, F. T. (1978). 'Incomes Policy' in Blackaby, F. T. (ed.), *British Economic Policy, 1960–74.* Cambridge University Press.

Booth, A. L. (1995). *The Economics of the Trade Union.* Cambridge University Press.

Booth, A. (1996). 'Corporate Politics and the Quest for Productivity: the British TUC and the Politics of Industrial Productivity, 1957–60' in J. Melling and A. McKinlay (eds.), *Management, Labour and Industrial Politics in Modern Europe,* Cheltenham, Edward Elgar, 1996.

Boston, S. (1980). *Women Workers and the Trade Unions.* London, Davis-Poynter. A useful survey of 1874–1975.

Broadberry, S. (1997). *The Productivity Race. British Manufacturing in International Perspective, 1850–1990.* Cambridge University Press.

Broadberry, S. and Howlett, P. (1998). 'The United Kingdom: "Victory at all Costs"' in Harrison, M. (ed.), *The Economics of World War II.* Cambridge University Press.

Brown, W. A. (1976). 'Incomes Policy and Pay Differentials'. *Oxford Bulletin of Economics and Statistics,* 38.

(1981). (ed.). *The Changing Contours of British Industrial Relations.* Oxford, Blackwell.

Bullock, Alan (1967). *The Life and Times of Ernest Bevin,* vol. 2. London, Heinemann.

Burchell, Brendan, Ladipo, David and Wilkinson, Frank (2002). *Job Insecurity and Work Intensification.* London, Routledge. Draws on the Joseph Rowntree Foundation surveys on white-collar work intensification in the 1990s.

Campbell, A., Fishman, N., and McIlroy, J. (eds.). (1999). *British Trade Unions and Industrial Politics: The Post-War Compromise 1945–64.* Aldershot, Ashgate.

Carter, B. (1986). 'Trade Unionism and the New Middle Class: The Case of ASTMS' in Armstrong, P., Carter, B., Smith, C. and Nichols, T. *White Collar Workers, Trade Unions and Class.* London, Croom Helm.

Charlesworth, Andrew, Gilbert, David, Randall, Adrian, Southall, Humphrey and Wrigley, Chris (1996). *An Atlas of Industrial Protest in Britain, 1750–1990.* London, Macmillan.

Church, R. and Outram, Q. (1998). *Strikes and Solidarity: Coalfield Conflict in Britain 1889–1966.* Cambridge University Press. A very impressive assessment.

Clegg, H. A. (1972). *The System of Industrial Relations in Great Britain.* Oxford, Blackwell.

(1976). *Trade Unions Under Collective Bargaining: A Theory Based on Comparisons of Six Countries.* Oxford, Blackwell.

(1983). 'Otto Kahn-Freund and British Industrial Relations' in Wedderburn, Lewis and Clark (eds.).

(1985). *A History of British Trade Unionism Since 1889*, vol. 2: *1911–33*. Oxford, Clarendon Press. The major history: detailed and reliable on facts.

(1994). *A History of British Trade Unionism Since 1889*, vol. 3: *1934–51*. Oxford, Clarendon Press. The major history: detailed and reliable on facts.

Clegg, H. A., Killick, A. J. and Adams, R. (1961). *Trade Union Officers*. Oxford, Blackwell.

Clinton, A. (1984). *Post Office Workers: A Trade Union and Social History*. Manchester University Press.

Coates, K. and Topham, T. (1986). *Trade Unions and Politics*. Oxford, Blackwell.

Court, W. B. (1951). *Coal*. London, HMSO.

Crafts, N. F. R. (1991). 'Economic Growth' in Crafts, N. F. R. and Woodward, N. (eds.). *The British Economy Since 1945*. Oxford, Clarendon Press.

Crompton, Rosemary (1997). *Women and Work in Modern Britain*. Oxford University Press. A useful introduction to its subject and to its author's important work.

Cronin, James (1979). *Industrial Conflict in Modern Britain*. London, Croom Helm. A major contribution to its subject.

Croucher, Richard (1982). *Engineers At War*. London, Merlin.

Cully, M., Woodland, S., O'Reilly, A. and Dix, G. (1999). *Britain At Work: As depicted by the 1998 Workplace Employee Relations Survey*. London, Routledge.

Daniel, W. and McIntosh, N. (1973). *Incomes Policy and Collective Bargaining at the Workplace*. London, Berridge.

Davies, P. and Freedland, M. (1993). *Labour Legislation and Public Policy: A Contemporary History*. Oxford, Clarendon Press.

Davies, R. J. (1963). 'Incomes and Anti-Inflation Policy' in Bain, G. S. (ed.), *Industrial Relations in Britain*. Oxford, Blackwell.

(1979). 'Economic Activity, Incomes Policy and Strikes: a quantitative analysis'. *British Journal of Industrial Relations*, 18.

Desai, T., Gregg, P., Steer, J. and Wadsworth, J. (1999). 'Gender and the Labour Market' in Gregg and Wadsworth (eds.).

Dickens, L. and Hall, M. (1995). 'The State: Labour Law and Industrial Relations' in Edwards (ed.).

Dorey, P. (1995). *The Conservative Party and the Trade Unions*. London, Routledge.

(2001). *Wage Politics in Britain*. Brighton, Sussex Academic Press.

Durcan, J. W., McCarthy, W. E. J. and Redman, G. P. (1983). *Strikes in Post-War Britain: A Study of Stoppages of Work due to Industrial Disputes, 1946–73*. London, Allen and Unwin. An important and influential analysis.

Edwards, Paul (ed.). (1995). *Industrial Relations: Theory and Practice in Britain*. Oxford, Blackwell.

Elgar, J. and Simpson, B. (1993). *Union Negotiators, Industrial Action and the Law: A Survey of Negotiators in Twenty-Five Unions, 1991–92*. London, LSE.

Employment, Department of (1968). *British Labour Statistics: Historical Abstract*. London, HMSO.

Evans, S. (1987). 'The Use of Injunctions in Industrial Disputes, May 1984–April 1987'. *British Journal of Industrial Relations*, 25.3.

Fallick, J. L. and Elliott, R. F. (eds.). (1981). *Incomes Policies, Inflation and Relative Pay*. London, Allen and Unwin. Still a useful collection of essays.

Fishbein, W. (1984). *Wage Restraint by Consensus: Britain's Search for an Incomes Policy Agreement, 1965–79*. London, Routledge and Kegan Paul.

Fishman, Nina (1995). *The British Communist Party and the Trade Unions 1933–45*. Aldershot, Scholar Press. The major study of its subject.

(1999). '"A Vital Element in British Industrial Relations": A Reassessment of Order 1305, 1940–51'. *Historical Studies in Industrial Relations*, 8, autumn 1999.

Flanagan, R. J., Soskice, D. W. and Ulman, L. (1983). *Unionism, Economic Stability and Incomes Policies*. Washington DC, Brookings Institute.

Flanders, A. (1964). *The Fawley Productivity Agreement*. London, Faber.

Fosh, P. and Heery, E. (1990). *Trade Unions and their Members*. London, Macmillan.

Freeman, R. B. and Medoff, J. L. (1984). *What Do Unions Do?* New York, Basic Books.

Fox, A. (1985). *History and Heritage: The Social Origins of the British Industrial Relations System*. London, Allen and Unwin. A valuable survey.

Gall, G. and MacKay, S. (1996). 'Injunctions as Legal Weapons in Industrial Disputes'. *British Journal of Industrial Relations*, 32.3.

Gallie, D., Penn, R. and Rose, M. (eds.). *Trade Unionism In Recession*. Oxford, Clarendon Press.

Gennard, J. and Bain, P. (1995). *A History of the Society of Graphical and Allied Trades*. London, Routledge.

Gilbert, David (1996a). 'Strikes in Post-War Britain' in Wrigley, 1996a.

(1996b). 'The Harworth Dispute of 1936–7' in Charlesworth, A. *et al.*

(1996c). 'The Geography of Strikes, 1940–90' in Charlesworth, A. *et al.*

Gilbert, Martin (1983). *Winston S. Churchill*, vol. 5 and Companion volumes. London, Heinemann.

Goldstein, Joseph (1952). *The Government of British Trade Unions*. London, Allen and Unwin.

Gregg, Paul and Wadsworth, J. (eds.). (1999). *The State of Working Britain*. Manchester University Press. Valuable survey of the British labour market at end of twentieth century.

Hakim, Catherine (1996). *Key Issues in Women's Work: Female Heterogeneity and the Polarisation of Women's Employment*. London, Athlone Press. A highly controversial yet challenging revisionist reassessment.

—— (1998). *Social Change and Innovation in the Labour Market*. Oxford University Press.

Hancock, W. K. and Gowing, M. (1949). *British War Economy*. London, HMSO.

Hanson, C. G. (1991). *Taming The Trade Unions: A Guide to the Thatcher Government's Employment Reforms, 1980–90*. London, Macmillan. Enthusiastic for the Thatcher legal reforms.

Heery, E. and Kelly, J. (1988). 'Do Female Representatives make a Difference? Women Full-time Officials and Trade Union Work'. *Work, Employment and Society*, 2.

Hinton, James (1994). *Shop Floor Citizens: Engineering Democracy In 1940s Britain*. Cheltenham, Edward Elgar. Detailed study of shop stewards and shop committees in Second World War and after.

Hunt, J. (1982). 'A Woman's Place is in her Union' in West, J. (ed.), *Work, Women and the Labour Market*. London, Routledge and Kegan Paul.

Hyman, Richard (1989). *Strikes*, 4th edition (1st edition, 1972). London, Macmillan.

Ingham, Geoffrey K. (1974). *Strikes and Industrial Conflict: Britain and Scandinavia*. London, Macmillan.

Inman, P. (1957). *Labour in the Munitions Industries*. London, HMSO.

Ironside, M. and Seifert, R. (2000). *Facing up to Thatcherism: The History of NALGO 1979–1993*. Oxford University Press.

Itzin, Catherine (1980). *Stages in the Revolution: Political Theatre in Britain since 1968*. London, Methuen.

Jackson, D., Turner, H. A. and Wilkinson, F. (1973). *Do Trade Unions Cause Inflation?* Cambridge University Press.

Jackson, M. P. (1987). *Strikes: Industrial Conflict in Britain, USA and Australia*. Brighton, Harvester Press.

Jenkins, Clive (1990). *All Against The Collar: Struggles of a White Collar Union Leader*. London, Methuen.

Jenkins, Clive and Sherman, B. (1979). *White-Collar Unionism: The Rebellious Salariat*. London, Routledge and Kegan Paul.

Jones, R. (1987). *Wages and Employment Policy 1936–1985*. London, Allen and Unwin. A lucid survey.

Jones, Stephen (1986). 'The British Trade Unions and Holidays With Pay', *International Review of Social History*, 31, pp. 40–67.

Kahn-Freund, O. (1954). 'Intergroup Conflicts and their Settlement', *British Journal of Sociology*, 5, 193.

Kelly, J. (2000). *Rethinking Industrial Relations*. London, Routledge.

Kelly, J. and Heery, E. (1994). *Working For The Union*. Cambridge University Press.

Kessler, Sid and Bayliss, Fred (1998). *Contemporary British Industrial Relations*, 3rd edition (1st edition, 1992). London, Macmillan. Very good surveys.

Knowles, K. G. C. (1952). *Strikes – A Study in Industrial Conflict*. Oxford, Blackwell. The classic work.

Latta, G. (1972). 'Trade Union Finances', *British Journal of Industrial Relations*, 10.2.

Laybourn, Keith (1992). *A History of British Trade Unionism*. Stroud, Sutton. A succinct and lucid history of 1770–1990.

Lewenhak, Sheila (1977). *Women and Trade Unions*. London, Benn.

Lindop, F. (2001). 'Racism and the Working Class: Strikes in Support of Enoch Powell in 1968'. *Labour History Review*, 66.1.

Lowe, R. (1987). 'The Government and Industrial Relations 1919–1939' in Wrigley (ed.).

Lunn, K. (1999). 'Complex Encounters: Trade Unions, Immigration and Race' in McIlroy, Fishman and Campbell (eds.).

Martin, R.M. (1980). *The TUC: The Growth of a Pressure Group, 1868–1976*. Oxford, Clarendon Press.

Mass Observation (1943). *War Factory*. London, Gollancz.

Mayhew, K. (1981). 'Incomes Policy and the Private Sector' in Fallick and Elliott (eds.).

McCarthy, W. E. J. (1966). *The Role of Shop Stewards in British Industrial Relations*, London, HMSO. The first research paper for the 1965–8 Royal Commission.

(1970). 'The Nature of Britain's Strike Problem'. *British Journal of Industrial Relations*, 8.

(1992). (ed.). *Legal Intervention in Industrial Relations: Gains and Losses*. Oxford, Blackwell. An important collection.

McCarthy, W. E. J. and Parker, S. R. (1968). *Shop Stewards and Workshop Relations*. London, HMSO. The tenth research paper for the 1965–8 Royal Commission.

McIlroy, John (1995). *Trade Unions in Britain Today*, 2nd edition. Manchester University Press.

(1997). 'Still Under Siege: British Trade Unions at the Turn of the Century' (Review essay). *Historical Studies in Industrial Relations*, 3.

McIlroy, J., Fishman, N. and Campbell, A. (eds.). (1999). *British Trade Unions and Industrial Politics: The High Tide of Trade Unionism, 1964–79*. Aldershot, Ashgate.

McInnes, John (1987). *Thatcherism At Work: Industrial Relations and Economic Change*. Milton Keynes, Open University.

Melling, Joseph (2002). 'Leadership and Factionalism in the Growth of Supervisory Trade-Unionism: The Case of ASSET, 1939–1956'. *Historical Studies in Industrial Relations*, 13 (spring 2002), 37–82.

Metcalf, D. (1988). 'Trade Unions and Economic Performance: The British Evidence'. *LSE Quarterly*, 3.

(1989). 'Water Notes Dry Up: The Impact of the Donovan Reform Proposals and Thatcherism at Work on Labour Productivity in British Manufacturing Industry'. *British Journal of Industrial Relations*, 27.

(1993). 'Industrial Relations and Economic Performance'. *British Journal of Industrial Relations*, 31.

Metcalf, D., Hansen, K. and Charlwood, A. (2000). *Unions and the Sword of Justice*. London, Centre for Economic Performance, London School of Economics.

Metcalf, D. and Milner, S. (eds.). (1993). *New Perspectives on Industrial Disputes*. London, Routledge.

Middlemas, Keith (1979). *Politics In Industrial Society*. London, Deutsch. The case for a corporatist interpretation of British politics, 1914–79.

Millward, N., Bryson, A. and Forth, J. (2000). *All Change At Work?* London, Routledge.

Mishel, L. and Voos, P. B. (1992). *Unions And Economic Competitiveness*. New York, M.E. Sharpe. A publication sponsored by The Economic Policy Institute, Washington DC.

Mitchell, Joan (1972). *The National Board for Prices and Incomes*. London, Seeker and Warburg.

Morgan, Kevin (1989). *Against Fascism and War: Ruptures and Continuities in British Communist Politics 1935–1941*. Manchester University Press.

OECD. (1986). *Compendium of Statistics and Indicators on the Situation of Women*. Paris, OECD.

Parker, H. M. D. (1957). *Manpower: A Study of War-time Policy and Administration*. London, HMSO.

Parker, R. A. C. (1981). 'British Rearmament 1936–39: Treasury, Trade Unions and Skilled Labour'. *English Historical Review*, April.

Pelling, Henry (1987). *A History of British Trade Unionism*, 4th edition. Harmondsworth, Penguin. A careful and mostly very reliable survey.

Phelps Brown, H. (1983). *The Origins of Trade Union Power*. Oxford University Press.

Phillips, A. W. (1958). 'The Relationship between Unemployment and the Rate of Change of Money Wages in the United Kingdom, 1861–1957'. Economica, November.

Prais, S. J. (1978). 'The strike-proneness of large plants in Britain'. *Journal of the Royal Statistical Society*, 141.

Rees, Teresa (1992). *Women and the Labour Market*. London, Routledge.

Roberts, B. C. (1956). *Trade Union government in Great Britain*. London, Bell.

Rookes, D. (1966). *Conspiracy*. London, Johnson.

Ross, Arthur, M. and Hartman, Paul T. (1960). *Changing Patterns of Industrial Conflict*. New York, John Wiley.

Rowbotham, S. and Tate, J. (1998). 'Homeworking: New Approaches to an Old Problem' in Drew, E., Emerek, R. and Mahon, E. (eds.). *Women, Work and the Family in Europe*. London, Routledge.

Royal Commission on Trade Unions and Employers' Associations (1968). *Report*. London, HMSO. (The Donovan Commission.)

Rubery, Jill (ed.). (1988). *Women and Recession*. London, Routledge and Kegan Paul.

(1998). 'Part-time Work: a Threat to Labour Standards?' in O'Reilly, J. and Fagan, C. (eds.), *Part-Time Prospects*. London, Routledge.

Russell, Alice (1991). *The Growth of Occupational Welfare in Britain*. Aldershot, Gower.

(1998). *The Harmonisation of Employment Conditions in Britain*. London, Macmillan.

Smith, C. T. B., Clifton, R., Makeham, P., Creigh, S. W. and Burns, R. V. (1978). *Strikes In Britain*. London, HMSO.

Smith, J. Davis (1990). *The Attlee and Churchill Administrations and Industrial Unrest 1945–55*. London, Pinter.

Smith, P. (1995). 'Change in British Trade Unions'. *Work, Employment and Society*, 9.1.

(1996). 'The Road Haulage Industry, 1945–79: From Statutory Regulation to Contested Terrain' in Wrigley (ed.).

(1997). 'The Road Haulage Industry 1918–1940'. *Historical Studies in Industrial Relations*, 3.

(1999). 'The "Winter of Discontent". The Hire and Reward Road Haulage Dispute, 1979'. *Historical Studies in Industrial Relations*, 7, spring.

Steele, R. (1981). 'Incomes Policy and Low Pay' in Fallick and Elliott (ed.).

Summerfield, Penny (1984). *Women Workers in the Second World War: Production and Patriarchy in Conflict*.

Supple, Barry (1987). *The History of the British Coal Industry, Vol. 4: The Political Economy of Decline*. Oxford, Clarendon Press.

Taylor, A. (1994). 'The Party and the Trade Unions' in Seldon, A. and Ball, S. (eds.), *The Conservative Century*. Oxford University Press.

(1999). 'The Conservative Party and the Trade Unions' in McIlroy, Fishman and Campbell (eds.).

Taylor, Robert (1993). *The Trade Union Question in British Politics*. Oxford, Blackwell. Excellent survey.

Terry, M. (1999). 'Systems of Collective Representation in Non-Union Firms in the UK'. *Industrial Relations Journal*, 30.1.

Tiratsoo, N. and Tomlinson, J. (1993). *State Intervention and Industrial Efficiency: Labour, 1939–1951*. London, Routledge.

Tomlinson, J. (1990). *Hayek and the Market*, London, Pluto.

(1991). 'A Lost Opportunity? Labour and the Productivity Problem' in Jones, G. and Kirby, M. W. (eds.), *Competitiveness and the State in Twentieth Century Britain*. Manchester University Press.

TUC (2001). *Focus on Industrial Action and Balloting*. London, TUC.

Turner, H. A. (1969). *Is Britain Really Strike-Prone?* Cambridge University Press.

Turner, H. A., Clack, G. and Roberts, B. C. (1987). *Labour Relations in the Motor Industry*. London, Allen and Unwin.

Undy, R. (1996). 'Mergers and Union Restructuring: Externally Determined Waves or Internally Generated Reforms?' *Historical Studies in Industrial Relations*, 2.

Undy, R., Ellis, V., McCarthy, W. E. J. and Halmos, A. M. (1981). *Change in the Trade Unions*. London, Hutchinson.

Waddington, J. (1988). 'Trade Union Mergers: A Study of Trade Union Structural Dynamics'. *British Journal of Industrial Relations*, 26.3.

(1992). 'Unemployment and Restructuring in Trade Union Membership in Britain 1980–87'. *British Journal of Industrial Relations*, 30.2.

(1995). *The Politics of Bargaining: The Merger Process and British Trade Union Structural Development 1892–1987*. London, Mansell.

(1997). 'External and Internal Influences on Union Mergers: A Response to Roger Undy'. *Historical Studies in Industrial Relations*, 3.

Waddington, J. and Whitston, C. (1995). 'Trade Unions, Growth, Structure and Policy' in Edwards (ed.).

Walby, S. (1986). *Patriarchy at Work: Patriarchal and Capitalist Relations in Employment*. London, Polity Press. A feminist analysis.

(1990). *Theorising Patriarchy*. Oxford, Blackwell.

Walsh, Kenneth (1983). *Strikes in Europe and the United States*. London, Frances Pinter.

Walsh, M. and Wrigley, C. J. (2001). 'Womanpower: The Transformation of the Labour Force in the UK and USA Since 1945'. *ReFRESH*, 30.

Watson, Jane (1988). *Managers of Discontent: Trade Union Officers and Industrial Relations Managers*. London, Routledge.

Wedderburn, Lord, Lewis, R. and Clark, J. (eds.). (1983). *Labour Law and Industrial Relations*. Oxford, Clarendon Press.

Weekes, B., Mellish, M., Dickens, L. and Lloyd, J. (1975). *Industrial Relations and the Limits of the Law: The Industrial Effects of the Industrial Relations Act, 1971*. Oxford, Blackwell.

Wesker, Arnold (1971). *Fear of Fragmentation*. London, Cape.

Western, Bruce (1997). *Between Class and Market. Postwar Unionization in the Capitalist Democracies*. Princeton University Press.

Willman, P., Morris, T. and Aston, B. (1993). *Union Business: Trade Union Organization and Financial Reform in the Thatcher Years*. Cambridge University Press. Oxford, Blackwell.

Worley, M. (2002). *Class Against Class*. London, I. B. Tauris. National and international dimensions of communism between the Wars.

Worswick, G. D. N. (1944). 'The Stability and Flexibility of Full Employment' in Oxford University Institute of Statistics, *The Economics of Full Employment*. Oxford, Blackwell.

Wrigley, Chris (1987). *A History of British Industrial Relations 1914–1939*. Brighton, Harvester Press.

(1991). 'Trade Unions, the Government and the Economy' in Gourvish, T. and O'Day, A. (eds.), *Britain Since 1945*. London, Macmillan.

(1996a). (ed.). *A History of British Industrial Relations 1939–1979*. Cheltenham, Edward Elgar.

(1996b). 'The Second World War and state intervention in industrial relations 1939–45' in Wrigley (ed.), 1996a.

(1996c). 'Trade Union development, 1945–79' in Wrigley (ed.), 1996a.

(1997). *British Trade Unions, 1945–1995*. Manchester University Press. In the series Documents in Contemporary History.

(1999a). 'From ASSET to ASTMS. An Example of White-Collar Union Growth in the 1960s'. *Historical Studies in Industrial Relations*, 7, spring.

(1999b). 'Women in the Labour Market and in the Unions' in McIlroy, Fishman and Campbell.

(2000). 'Organized labour and the international economy' in Wrigley, Chris (ed.), *The First World War and the International Economy*. Cheltenham, Edward Elgar.

(2001). 'Churchill and the Trade Unions'. *Transactions of the Royal Historical Society*, sixth series, 11.

Index

New Studies in Economic and Social History

Titles in the series available from Cambridge University Press:

13. A. Dyer, *Decline and Growth in English Towns 1400–1640*
    ISBN 0 521 55272 9 (hardback) 0 521 55781 X (paperback)

14. R. B. Outhwaite, *Dearth, Public Policy and Social Disturbance in England, 1550–1800*
    ISBN 0 521 55273 7 (hardback) 0 521 55780 1 (paperback)

15. M. Sanderson, *Education, Economic Change and Society in England*
    ISBN 0 521 55274 5 (hardback) 0 521 55779 8 (paperback)

16. R. D. Anderson, *Universities and Elites in Britain since 1800*
    ISBN 0 521 55275 3 (hardback) 0 521 55778 X (paperback)

17. C. Heywood, *The Development of the French Economy, 1700–1914*
    ISBN 0 521 55276 1 (hardback) 0 521 55777 1 (paperback)

18. R. A. Houston, *The Population History of Britain and Ireland 1500–1750*
    ISBN 0 521 55277 X (hardback) 0 521 55776 3 (paperback)

19. A. J. Reid, *Social Classes and Social Relations in Britain 1850–1914*
    ISBN 0 521 55278 8 (hardback) 0 521 55775 5 (paperback)

20. R. Woods, *The Population of Britain in the Nineteenth Century*
    ISBN 0 521 55279 6 (hardback) 0 521 55774 7 (paperback)

21. T. C. Barker, *The Rise and Rise of Road Transport, 1700–1990*
    ISBN 0 521 55280 X (hardback) 0 521 55773 9 (paperback)

22. J. Harrison, *The Spanish Economy*
    ISBN 0 521 55281 8 (hardback) 0 521 55772 0 (paperback)

23. C. Schmitz, *The Growth of Big Business in the United States and Western Europe, 1850–1939*
    ISBN 0 521 55282 6 (hardback) 0 521 55771 2 (paperback)

24. R. A. Church, *The Rise and Decline of the British Motor Industry*
    ISBN 0 521 55283 4 (hardback) 0 521 55770 4 (paperback)

25. P. Horn, *Children's Work and Welfare, 1780–1880*
    ISBN 0 521 55284 2 (hardback) 0 521 55769 0 (paperback)

26. R. Perren, *Agriculture in Depression, 1870–1940*
    ISBN 0 521 55285 0 (hardback) 0 521 55768 2 (paperback)

27. R. J. Overy, *The Nazi Economic Recovery 1932–1938* (second edition)
    ISBN 0 521 55286 9 (hardback) 0 521 55767 4 (paperback)

28. S. Cherry, *Medical Services and the Hospitals in Britain, 1860–1939*
    ISBN 0 521 57126 X (hardback) 0 521 57784 5 (paperback)

29. D. Edgerton, *Science, Technology and the British Industrial 'Decline', 1870–1970*
    ISBN 0 521 57127 8 (hardback) 0 521 57778 0 (paperback)

30. C. A. Whatley, *The Industrial Revolution in Scotland*
ISBN 0 521 57228 2 (hardback) 0 521 57643 1 (paperback)

31. H. E. Meller, *Towns, Plans and Society in Modern Britain*
ISBN 0 521 57227 4 (hardback) 0 521 57644 X (paperback)

32. H. Hendrick, *Children, Childhood and English Society, 1880–1990*
ISBN 0 521 57253 3 (hardback) 0 521 57624 5 (paperback)

33. N. Tranter, *Sport, Economy and Society in Britain, 1750–1914*
ISBN 0 521 57217 7 (hardback) 0 521 57655 5 (paperback)

34. R. W. Davies, *Soviet Economic Development from Lenin to Khrushchev*
ISBN 0 521 62260 3 (hardback) 0 521 62742 7 (paperback)

35. H. V. Bowen, *War and British Society, 1688–1815*
ISBN 0 521 57226 6 (hardback) 0 521 57645 8 (paperback)

36. M. M. Smith, *Debating Slavery in the Antebellum American South*
ISBN 0 521 57158 8 (hardback) 0 521 57696 2 (paperback)

37. M. Sanderson, *Education and Economic Decline in Britain, 1870 to the 1990s*
ISBN 0 521 58170 2 (hardback) 0 521 58842 1 (paperback)

38. V. Berridge, *Health Policy, Health and Society, 1939 to the 1990s*
ISBN 0 521 57230 4 (hardback) 0 521 57641 5 (paperback)

39. M. E. Mate, *Women in Medieval English Society*
ISBN 0 521 58322 5 (hardback) 0 521 58733 6 (paperback)

40. P. J. Richardson, *Economic Change in China, c. 1800–1950*
ISBN 0 521 58396 9 (hardback) 0 521 63571 3 (paperback)

41. J. E. Archer, *Social Unrest and Popular Protest in England, 1780–1840*
ISBN 0 521 57216 9 (hardback) 0 521 57656 3 (paperback)

42. K. Morgan, *Slavery, Atlantic Trade and British Economy, 1660–1800*
ISBN 0 521 58213 X (hardback) 0 521 58814 6 (paperback)

43. C. W. Chalklin, *The Rise of the English Town, 1650–1850*
ISBN 0 521 66141 2 (hardback) 0 521 66737 2 (paperback)

44. J. Cohen and G. Federico, *The Growth of the Italian Economy, 1820–1960*
ISBN 0 521 66150 1 (hardback) 0 521 66692 9 (paperback)

45. T. Balderston, *Economics and Politics in the Weimar Republic*
ISBN 0 521 58375 6 (hardback) 0 521 77760 7 (paperback)

46. C. Wrigley, *British Trade Unions since 1933*
ISBN 0 521 57231 2 (hardback) 0 521 57640 7 (paperback)

47. A. Colli, *Family Business in Historical and Comparative Perspective*
ISBN 0 521 80028 5 (hardback) 0 521 80472 8 (paperback)

Previously published as

Studies in Economic and Social History

Titles in the series available from the Macmillan Press Limited:

Economic History Society

The Economic History Society, which numbers around 3,000 members, publishes the quarterly *Economic History Review* (free to members) and holds an annual conference.

Enquiries about membership should be addressed to:

The Assistant Secretary
Economic History Society
PO Box 70
Kingswood
Bristol
BS15 5TB

Full-time students may join at special rates.